Reading Achievement

Comprehension Activities to Promote Essential Reading Skills

Grade 8

by

Darriel Ledbetter, M.S.

and

Leland Graham, Ph.D.

Table of Contents

Introduction

Welcome to the **Reading Achievement** series! Each book in this series is designed to reinforce the reading skills appropriate for each grade level and to encourage high-level thinking skills. Because reading is an essential part of all disciplines, mastery of these skills can help students succeed in all academic areas. In addition, experiencing success in reading can increase a student's self-esteem and motivate him or her to read more, both in and out of the classroom.

Each **Reading Achievement** book offers challenging questions for students to answer in response to a variety of grade-level appropriate passages. Various types of reading passages are represented in this book, including fiction, nonfiction, poetry, letters, maps, charts and graphs, and recipes. The format and questions are similar to those found on standardized reading tests. The experience students gain from answering questions in this format may help increase their test scores. In addition, these exercises can be used to enhance your school-adopted reading program, to individualize instruction, to provide extra practice for home schoolers, or to review skills between grades.

The following reading skills are covered within this book:

- **compare and contrast**
- **comprehension**
- **critical thinking**
- **figurative language**
- **following directions**
- **main ideas/details**
- **reference skills**
- **sequencing**
- **vocabulary**
- **true or false**

Each **Reading Achievement** book contains additional features to enhance usability. Four pretests, in standardized test format, have been included at the beginning of each book. The pretests have been designed so that they may be used individually, as four stand-alone tests, or in groups. Another convenient feature is a scoring box on each activity page. This scoring box can be programmed to suit your specific classroom and student needs with total problems, total correct, and score.

Name ______________________________ **Pretest**

Read the passage. Circle the letter beside each correct answer.

Many of us like to collect seashells when we visit the beach. Did you know that seashells are the coverings of soft-bodied sea animals? Usually when we find them on the beach they are empty. The animals that lived in them have been washed out as the shell was tumbled by the ocean waves. These animals belong to a large group of animals called **mollusks**.

People have used seashells in different ways. Some Native Americans used them as money, which was called **wampum**. Mother-of-pearl is a smooth, shiny layer inside some shells, which is used for buttons and jewelry.

Bivalves are common, two-shelled mollusks. Each shell is joined to the other at a hinge. Oysters, scallops, mussels, and clams are bivalves. Collectors like these shells because of their color and design.

Sea snails are a large group of mollusks. Most of these have a single, spiral shell. Because many of the most beautiful shells belong to this group, they are the most **prized** by collectors. Members of this group are the *limpet*, *top shell*, *turban shell*, *cowry*, *conch*, and *whelk*.

Tusk shells look like small elephant tusks. They are hollow, curved shells that are bigger at one end. Sometimes they are called tooth shells.

1. This selection is about:
   A. mollusks B. mammals C. valves D. ocean creatures

2. In the second paragraph, the word **wampum** means:
   A. jewelry B. weapon C. award D. money

3. Which is **not** a member of the mollusk family?
   A. limpet B. oyster C. shrimp D. mussel

4. Bivalves have how many shells?
   A. one B. two C. four D. one hollow one

5. In the third paragraph, the word **prized** means:
   A. large B. desired C. expensive D. beautiful

6. Collectors are most interested in sea snail shells because of their:
   A. size B. beauty C. usefulness D. flavor

7. Tusk shells are probably called this because of:
   A. their use B. cost C. appearance D. color

8. Seashells are actually:
   A. pieces of rock B. bones C. sand D. coverings of sea animals

Total Problems: **Total Correct:** **Score:**

Name ______________________________ **Pretest**

Refer to the graph to answer the questions. Circle the letter beside each correct answer.

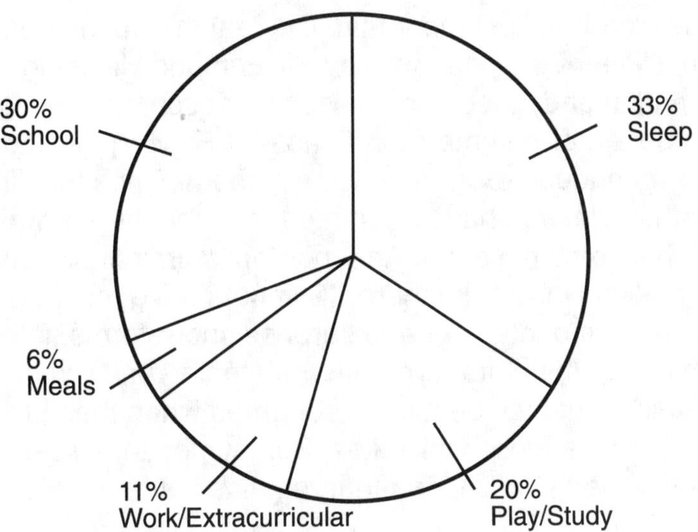

1. What does this graph show?
   A. a teenager's use of money
   B. a teenager's use of time
   C. a teenager's vacation schedule
   D. a teenager's favorite subject

2. What percent does the entire circle represent?
   A. 50% B. 75% C. 100% D. 105%

3. According to this graph, a teenager spends the greatest amount of time in which activity?
   A. play/study B. work/extracurricular C. school D. sleep

4. According to this graph, a teenager spends the least amount of time in which activity?
   A. play/study B. work/extracurricular C. school D. meals

5. According to this graph, a teenager spends more than half his day in which two activities?
   A. meals and sleep
   B. work/extracurricular and meals
   C. sleep and school
   D. play/study and school

6. According to this graph, a teenager spends **about** twice as much time in play and study as which other activity?
   A. school B. work/extracurricular C. meals D. school

7. If the data in this graph were converted to a bar graph, which bar would be the longest?
   A. sleep B. work/extracurricular C. school D. play/study

8. Another name for a circle graph is:
   A. pie graph B. ring graph C. line graph D. sphere

Total Problems:	**Total Correct:**	**Score:**

Name ________________________________ **Pretest**

Read the passage. Circle the letter beside each correct answer.

Climbing Mt. Everest, the world's tallest mountain, is a feat that many people continue to attempt. The first successful climb of the peak was by Sir Edmund Hillary in 1953. Tenzing Norgay, a Sherpa from Nepal, who had already tried unsuccessfully, accompanied him. As they climbed, they endured bitter cold temperatures—some as cold as –27˚F; howling winds, and oxygen shortages, for it was difficult to carry enough oxygen tanks with them. Since this first successful expedition on Mt. Everest, many other climbers have attempted to reach the **summit** of the mountain. Many have been victorious, but some have not. And, perhaps surprisingly, once one reaches the top of the mountain, it is not "all downhill from there." Climbers have reached the top, only to perish on the return trip down the mountain, due to surprise snowstorms, falls, illness and injury, and lack of oxygen in the thin air. When the oxygen in their tanks runs low or runs out, climbers not only have difficulty breathing, but they become disoriented when their brains don't get enough oxygen, which causes them to make foolish mistakes. Sometimes the ascent has left climbers so weakened that they cannot survive the challenge that remains in the descent.

1. The main idea of this selection is:
- A. Attempting to climb Mt. Everest is difficult and can be dangerous.
- B. No one ever reaches the top of Mt. Everest the first time they try.
- C. One should try to climb Mt. Everest in the summer.
- D. The only difficult part of climbing Mt. Everest is going up.

2. Which of the following is not mentioned as a problem that climbers endure?
A. lack of oxygen B. bitter cold C. lack of food D. howling winds

3. In this selection the word **summit** means:
A. flag B. climb C. camp D. highest point

4. In this selection the phrase "all downhill from there" means:
A. easy B. sloping C. slick D. dangerous

5. Why must climbers carry oxygen tanks with them on the climb?
A. They have asthma. B. The air is too cold to breathe.
C. The air is so thin. D. The winds are so strong.

6. Lack of oxygen is an especially serious problem because in addition to making it difficult to breathe, it can cause a climber to:
A. fall B. go blind C. get sick D. make mistakes

7. The first successful climb of Mt. Everest was led by:
A. Sir Tenzing Norgay B. Mr. Sherpa from Nepal
C. Sir Edmund Hillary D. an anonymous climber

Total Problems: **Total Correct:** **Score:**

Name ______________________________ **Pretest**

Read the passage. Circle the letter beside each correct answer.

Mary Bass of Harlan, North Dakota, feels that she had more than her share of crisis situations—all within two days!

It all started when Mary tripped over a pair of her son's shoes that he had left in the middle of the den floor and had to go to the hospital for stitches. She also had a concussion. While she was in the hospital, a 15-year-old, who had never driven, stole a car and crashed into Mary's mini-van. It was totaled. When she was released from the hospital, her friend Jan took her to the grocery store and helped her get some things that would be easy to prepare for dinner. When Jan pulled into the driveway at home, she accidentally turned too soon and knocked down Mary's mailbox! Mary resisted the urge to cry and began cooking dinner. Fortunately, Jan's husband was very handy, and by dinner time, he had the mailbox looking better than new.

1. How long did Mary's crisis spree last?
   A. a week B. two weeks C. two days D. two hours

2. What was Mary's <u>second</u> crisis experience?
   A. She tripped over her son's shoes.
   B. Her friend ran over her mailbox.
   C. She fainted in the grocery store.
   D. A 15-year-old totaled her mini-van.

3. In this selection, the word **totaled** means:
   A. hit B. ruined C. added up D. sold

4. How might Mary's son have felt about Mary's first accident?
   A. guilty, because he should have put his shoes away
   B. angry, because his mom ruined his shoes
   C. like his mom should have been watching where she was going
   D. It really wasn't such a big deal.

5. Since Mary had a **concussion** and needed stitches, she probably injured what part of her body when she fell over her son's shoes?
   A. her knee B. her elbow C. her head D. her back

6. What happened to the 15-year-old who ran into Mary's mini-van?
   A. She said she was sorry.
   B. She went to school.
   C. She went to jail.
   D. You can't tell from the story.

7. When the mailbox was damaged, how did Mary feel?
   A. like laughing B. like crying C. strong D. energetic

Total Problems: Total Correct: Score:

Pretest Answer Key

Name ______________________ **Pretest**

Read the passage. Circle the letter beside each correct answer.

Many of us like to collect seashells when we visit the beach. Did you know that seashells are the coverings of soft-bodied sea animals? Usually when we find them on the beach they are empty. The animals that lived in them have been washed out as the shell was tumbled by the ocean waves. These animals belong to a large group of animals called **mollusks**.

People have used seashells in different ways. Some Native Americans used them as money, which was called **wampum**. Mother-of-pearl is a smooth, shiny layer inside some shells, which is used for buttons and jewelry.

Bivalves are common, two-shelled mollusks. Each shell is joined to the other at a hinge. Oysters, scallops, mussels, and clams are bivalves. Collectors like these shells because of their color and design.

Sea snails are a large group of mollusks. Most of these have a single, spiral shell. Because many of the most beautiful shells belong to this group, they are the most **prized** by collectors. Members of this group are the *limpet, top shell, turban shell, cowry, conch,* and *whelk.*

Tusk shells look like small elephant tusks. They are hollow, curved shells that are bigger at one end. Sometimes they are called tooth shells.

1. This selection is about:
   (A.) mollusks B. mammals C. valves D. ocean creatures
2. In the second paragraph, the word **wampum** means:
   A. jewelry B. weapon C. award (D.) money
3. Which is **not** a member of the mollusk family?
   A. limpet B. oyster (C.) shrimp D. mussel
4. Bivalves have how many shells?
   A. one (B.) two C. four D. one hollow one
5. In the third paragraph, the word **prized** means:
   A. large (B.) desired C. expensive D. beautiful
6. Collectors are most interested in sea snail shells because of their:
   A. size (B.) beauty C. usefulness D. flavor
7. Tusk shells are probably called this because of:
   A. their use B. cost (C.) appearance D. color
8. Seashells are actually:
   A. pieces of rock B. bones C. sand (D.) coverings of sea animals

Total Problems: Total Correct: Score:

Name ______________________ **Pretest**

Refer to the graph to answer the questions. Circle the letter beside each correct answer.

30% School
33% Sleep
6% Meals
11% Work/Extracurricular
20% Play/Study

1. What does this graph show?
   A. a teenager's use of money (B.) a teenager's use of time
   C. a teenager's vacation schedule D. a teenager's favorite subject
2. What percent does the entire circle represent?
   A. 50% B. 75% (C.) 100% D. 105%
3. According to this graph, a teenager spends the greatest amount of time in which activity?
   A. play/study B. work/extracurricular C. school (D.) sleep
4. According to this graph, a teenager spends the least amount of time in which activity?
   A. play/study B. work/extracurricular C. school (D.) meals
5. According to this graph, a teenager spends more than half his day in which two activities?
   A. meals and sleep B. work/extracurricular and meals
   (C.) sleep and school D. play/study and school
6. According to this graph, a teenager spends **about** twice as much time in play and study as which other activity?
   A. school (B.) work/extracurricular C. meals D. school
7. If the data in this graph were converted to a bar graph, which bar would be the longest?
   (A.) sleep B. work/extracurricular C. school D. play/study
8. Another name for a circle graph is:
   (A.) pie graph B. ring graph C. line graph D. sphere

Total Problems: Total Correct: Score:

Name ______________________ **Pretest**

Read the passage. Circle the letter beside each correct answer.

Climbing Mt. Everest, the world's tallest mountain, is a feat that many people continue to attempt. The first successful climb of the peak was by Sir Edmund Hillary in 1953. Tenzing Norgay, a Sherpa from Nepal, who had already tried unsuccessfully, accompanied him. As they climbed, they endured bitter cold temperatures—some as cold as –27°F; howling winds, and oxygen shortages, for it was difficult to carry enough oxygen tanks with them. Since this first successful expedition on Mt. Everest, many other climbers have attempted to reach the **summit** of the mountain. Many have been victorious, but some have not. And, perhaps surprisingly, once one reaches the top of the mountain, it is not "all downhill from there." Climbers have reached the top, only to perish on the return trip down the mountain, due to surprise snowstorms, falls, illness and injury, and lack of oxygen in the thin air. When the oxygen in their tanks runs low or runs out, climbers not only have difficulty breathing, but they become disoriented when their brains don't get enough oxygen, which causes them to make foolish mistakes. Sometimes the ascent has left climbers so weakened that they cannot survive the challenge that remains in the descent.

1. The main idea of this selection is:
   (A.) Attempting to climb Mt. Everest is difficult and can be dangerous.
   B. No one ever reaches the top of Mt. Everest the first time they try.
   C. One should try to climb Mt. Everest in the summer.
   D. The only difficult part of climbing Mt. Everest is going up.
2. Which of the following is not mentioned as a problem that climbers endure?
   A. lack of oxygen B. bitter cold (C.) lack of food D. howling winds
3. In this selection the word **summit** means:
   A. flag B. climb C. camp (D.) highest point
4. In this selection the phrase "all downhill from there" means:
   (A.) easy B. sloping C. slick D. dangerous
5. Why must climbers carry oxygen tanks with them on the climb?
   A. They have asthma. B. The air is too cold to breathe.
   (C.) The air is so thin. D. The winds are so strong.
6. Lack of oxygen is an especially serious problem because in addition to making it difficult to breathe, it can cause a climber to:
   A. fall B. go blind C. get sick (D.) make mistakes
7. The first successful climb of Mt. Everest was led by:
   A. Sir Tenzing Norgay B. Mr. Sherpa from Nepal
   (C.) Sir Edmund Hillary D. an anonymous climber

Total Problems: Total Correct: Score:

Name ______________________ **Pretest**

Read the passage. Circle the letter beside each correct answer.

Mary Bass of Harlan, North Dakota, feels that she had more than her share of crisis situations—all within two days!

It all started when Mary tripped over a pair of her son's shoes that he had left in the middle of the den floor and had to go to the hospital for stitches. She also had a concussion. While she was in the hospital, a 15-year-old, who had never driven, stole a car and crashed into Mary's mini-van. It was totaled. When she was released from the hospital, her friend Jan took her to the grocery store and helped her get some things that would be easy to prepare for dinner. When Jan pulled into the driveway at home, she accidentally turned too soon and knocked down Mary's mailbox! Mary resisted the urge to cry and began cooking dinner. Fortunately, Jan's husband was very handy, and by dinner time, he had the mailbox looking better than new.

1. How long did Mary's crisis spree last?
   A. a week B. two weeks (C.) two days D. two hours
2. What was Mary's <u>second</u> crisis experience?
   A. She tripped over her son's shoes. B. Her friend ran over her mailbox.
   C. She fainted in the grocery store. (D.) A 15-year-old totaled her mini-van.
3. In this selection, the word **totaled** means:
   A. hit (B.) ruined C. added up D. sold
4. How might Mary's son have felt about Mary's first accident?
   (A.) guilty, because he should have put his shoes away
   B. angry, because his mom ruined his shoes
   C. like his mom should have been watching where she was going
   D. It really wasn't such a big deal.
5. Since Mary had a **concussion** and needed stitches, she probably injured what part of her body when she fell over her son's shoes?
   A. her knee B. her elbow (C.) her head D. her back
6. What happened to the 15-year-old who ran into Mary's mini-van?
   A. She said she was sorry. B. She went to school.
   C. She went to jail. (D.) You can't tell from the story.
7. When the mailbox was damaged, how did Mary feel?
   A. like laughing (B.) like crying C. strong D. energetic

Total Problems: Total Correct: Score:

Name ____________________ **Following Directions**

Refer to the U.S. map to answer each question. Write your answers in the spaces provided.

1. In which direction would you travel if you went from Kentucky to Utah? ____________

2. Which two states are directly east of California? ____________

3. Which state is north of North Carolina? ____________

4. Name the states that border Minnesota on the west. ____________

5. Which state is between Mississippi and Georgia? ____________

6. Which two states are directly south of New York? ____________

7. In which direction would you travel to go from New Mexico to Wisconsin? ____________

8. Which three states border Louisiana? ____________

Total Problems: **Total Correct:** **Score:**

Name ______________________________

Read each passage. Circle the letter beside each correct answer.

The Flute

The flute, one of the oldest instruments ever created, has been around for the last several hundred years. The word *flute* is derived from the Latin word *flatus* which means "blowing" or "breathing." Playing the flute takes more air to make a sound than any other instrument. A person may often feel faint because of the amount of air needed to produce a good tone. However, this is a normal occurrence for any flautist seeking a balanced tone.

The tone of a flute is the most admired because it does not have a "squeak" or "honk" as does a clarinet or trumpet. At times, the flute may produce a high-pitched tone which is often described as sounding like a bird and is the most difficult tone to produce successfully. Other times the flute may produce a low-pitched tone, which is the most beautiful tone the flute makes. This type of musicality is most often used in music written in a minor key. Flute music can be the most enjoyable and the most challenging to play.

1. The main idea of the passage is that:
   A. The flute has been around for hundreds of years.
   B. The word "flute" comes from the word "flatus" which means "blowing."
   C. Flute music can be most enjoyable and the most challenging to play.
   D. At times, the flute sounds like a bird.

Nuclear Energy

According to the Nuclear Energy Institute, nuclear energy has perhaps the lowest impact on the environment of any energy source. Nuclear energy does not emit harmful gases; it isolates its waste from the environment and requires less area to produce the same amount of electricity as other sources. The long periods of operation and the large size of the plants have enabled United States nuclear energy plants to provide a dependable and economical source of electricity for the United States and the world. Unlike some other energy sources, nuclear energy is not subject to unreliable weather or climate conditions, or dependence on foreign suppliers.

2. The main idea of this paragraph is that:
   A. Nuclear power is an amazing accomplishment.
   B. Nuclear power needs a large supply of water to cool nuclear components.
   C. Nuclear power plants are built near lakes, rivers, or oceans.
   D. Nuclear energy is a safe, economical, and dependable source of electricity.

Total Problems: **Total Correct:** **Score:**

Read each passage. Circle the letter beside each correct answer.

Baseball

Baseball is one of the oldest and most popular spectator sports. During the early 1800s, baseball developed into the game it is today. Although its exact origins are obscure, it is thought by many to have been invented in 1839 by Abner Doubleday. He was a Union officer in the American Civil War. However, it more likely evolved from a popular eighteenth century English game called "rounders." Baseball became popular during the American Civil War, among both Northern and Southern troops.

The Cincinnati Red Stockings was the first professional baseball team and began play in 1869. Later, a separate league for black athletes produced many fine players in the early twentieth century. Jackie Robinson began playing for the Brooklyn Dodgers in 1947. This opened the doors for the racial integration of major-league baseball. He was one of the greatest players in the Negro Baseball Leagues and the first African-American player to play in the modern major leagues.

1. The main idea of this passage is:

A. Baseball may have been by invented civil war troops.
B. Baseball more likely evolved from "rounders," a Brooklyn game.
C. The passage relates the possible origins and history of major-league baseball.
D. Jackie Robinson opened the door for racial integration in baseball.

Disorders of Eating

Using food to meet emotional needs is a learned behavior that can become addictive and lead to disordered eating habits. There are several different types of eating disorders. These include *anorexia nervosa*—an extreme food restriction, and *bulimia nervosa*—a cycle of binge eating followed by vomiting, laxatives, or excessive exercise to get rid of food. Other types include *food addiction*—eating when not hungry, and *disordered eating*—an unbalanced attitude about food, weight, and the body that leads to very rigid eating and exercise habits. People can gain freedom from these learned behaviors by retraining themselves to use food to meet only physical needs and by learning healthy ways to satisfy their emotional needs.

2. The main idea of this passage is:

A. Disordered eating is a balanced attitude about food and the body.
B. Disordered eating is a learned behavior which can be unlearned.
C. Proper dieting and exercise is important.
D. Binge eating is unhealthy.

Total Problems: Total Correct: Score:

Read each passage. Circle the letter beside each correct answer.

An *inference* is an assumption based on the facts and evidence that are given.

Organ Transplants

There are over 60,000 people awaiting organ donations in the United States alone. The need for organ donations is urgent! There is a new name added to the organ transplant waiting list every sixteen minutes. This means ninety people a day and 32,850 people a year are being added to the waiting list. Living in this fast-paced world is a contributing factor to the increasing number of people awaiting transplants. This fast-paced lifestyle leads to the consumption of a poor diet which contributes to declining health. Stress can also be a major factor in the inability to fight disease. Together, these factors lead to the need for more organ transplants.

1. After reading the passage, one can infer that:

A. A poor diet can contribute to declining health.

B. Stress is a factor in the reduced ability to fight disease.

C. If stress and a fast-paced lifestyle are absent, the chances of needing an organ transplant are reduced.

D. Over 60,000 people are awaiting organ donations.

The Human Brain

The human brain controls bodily functions efficiently. Most health professionals believe that a positive attitude can boost a person's immune system. People can choose to practice either a positive or negative outlook. Optimism will yield a healthier person, just as a negative outlook can result in an unhealthy person. The brain has a major influence on bodily function; therefore, feelings, emotions, and states of mind have a major effect on the body's well-being.

2. An inference in the passage above is that:

A. The body controls the thinking process.

B. Immunity is acquired only after one has all the shots required.

C. The body controls feelings, emotions, and states of mind.

D. If a person has a positive attitude, the mind and body work together more efficiently.

Total Problems: **Total Correct:** **Score:**

Name ______________________________

Read each passage. Circle the letter beside each correct answer.

An *inference* is an assumption based on the facts and evidence that are given.

Peer Pressure

It is a common misconception that all peer pressure is negative. Some peer pressure is actually beneficial to adolescents. Peers are necessary in helping adolescents make a successful transition from dependency on their parents to self-reliance. Peers can and do act as positive role models. Peers can and do demonstrate appropriate social behaviors. Peers often listen to, accept, and understand the frustrations and challenges associated with being a teenager.

Peer pressure plays a beneficial part in every adolescent's development and involvement with others. Parents play a big part in helping the adolescent with the transition from dependency to independence. Parents can make sure that their child does not fall under the influence of a detrimental peer group. They can create strong bonds with their child, build the child's self-esteem, take an interest in what their child does, and set good examples.

1. An inference found in the second paragraph above is that:

A. If kids have strong, supportive parents, peer pressure will most likely be positive.
B. Parents cannot help that much in the transition from teenager to adult.
C. Peer pressure is necessary, but not so positive.
D. Peers often listen to concerns associated with being a teenager.

Obsessive-Compulsive Disorder

Obsessive-compulsive disorder, also known as OCD, is a biologically based anxiety disorder. This disorder can begin in childhood and persist throughout a person's life. The individual who suffers from OCD sometimes has thoughts of a disturbing nature, which may cause the person to repeat certain activities in an attempt to relieve anxiety. Symptomatic of the disorder are unwelcome thoughts and a compulsion to carry out meaningless rituals, such as guarding against danger or excessive cleaning. The paradox is that those with the disorder realize the rituals are irrational, yet find themselves repeating them in an effort to relieve anxiety. These symptoms can interfere with thinking, reasoning, and/or life functioning. Medical science has developed drug therapies and behavior modification techniques that have helped people with this disorder.

2. An inference you can make is that:

A. Obsessive-compulsive disorder is a mild childhood disorder.
B. Obsessive-compulsive disorder may begin only in one's adult life.
C. We often find ourselves in ordinary situations.
D. Someone who is obsessed with cleaning or guarding against danger may have OCD.

Total Problems:	Total Correct:	Score:

Name ___________________________

As you read the letter, keep in mind the clues that let you know the order in which the events happen. Then, circle the letter beside each correct answer.

Dear Jay,

I have been at Camp Mountain Lake for three weeks, but already it seems much longer. There have been so many activities and fun things to do that time has passed very quickly. I apologize for not having written sooner, but I haven't had much spare time.

The seventh- and eighth-grade boys are living in the Pioneer cabins this summer—quite different from last summer. Do you remember last summer? As a Pioneer, we are allowed a later curfew, and we are allowed to water-ski. You should be here. Terry Schwartz, a Cub from North Miami, fell last week on an overnight camping trip and broke his arm. The Cubs had gone camping in Pisgah, where we went last summer, and they were swimming and playing at Sliding Rock when he slipped and fell. That place is so much fun. I wore out the bottoms of two pairs of jeans there last summer, and this summer the Pioneers have been there once. I could spend a week there sliding down those rocks into the frigid icy water. The water must be around 32 degrees. Wouldn't you agree?

Tonight is the big bonfire on the hill where we did our outdoor drama last summer. Every cabin must participate in tonight's event. Do you remember the play last year? It was hilarious.

Write me when you get a chance. I will be home in about five weeks, and we will do some cool things before school begins. I must go and prepare for tonight.

Your friend,
Spencer

1. Which one of the following events happened first?
   A. . . . and they were swimming and playing at Sliding Rock when he slipped and fell.
   B. . . . fell last week on an overnight camping trip and broke his arm.
   C. Tonight is the big bonfire.
   D. Every cabin must participate in tonight's event.

2. Which one of the following events happened last?
   A. Terry Schwartz fell last week on an overnight camping trip and broke his arm.
   B. I wore out two pairs of jeans.
   C. . . . we will do some cool things before school begins.
   D. . . . where we went last summer, and they were swimming and playing . . .

Total Problems: **Total Correct:** **Score:**

As you read the passage, keep in mind the clues that let you know the order in which the events happen. Then, circle the letter beside each correct answer.

Just in Time

After a week of working hard and making friends in the town of Carmen Bajo, we took a day to explore the shops of Otavalo. After three hours of riding, we were all ready to take a walk, but not quite like the one I was about to take when I jumped off the bus into the busy streets of Quito, Ecuador.

It was just before dark when I looked up to see a cute, young boy who said his brother wanted to see me. I saw in his hand my address, in my own writing, and I realized who my little visitor must be. He was the brother of my friend, Fernando, who had come to visit me on my last night there.

Fernando walked around the block to find a taxi for his brother; we then decided to take a different route back. After walking for a while, we realized that this was not the road we were looking for. We were definitely lost! We ran for a while because I did not want to be late, especially since I was not supposed to have left the hotel in the first place, much less with a boy. Finally, we saw a police officer standing on a street corner, and he directed us to the hotel. When we could see the hotel down the road, we said our good-byes until next year, and I walked back to the hotel just in time. Everything had worked out perfectly; that is, until I looked down to see I was still holding his jacket, and he had already gotten into a taxi and disappeared.

1. Which one of the following events happened first?

A. Everything had worked out perfectly; that is, until I looked down to see . . .
B. After three hours of riding, we were all ready to take a walk . . .
C. We ran for a while because I did not want to be late, especially since I was . . .
D. We saw a police officer standing on a street corner, and he directed us to the hotel.

2. Which one of the following events happened last?

A. . . . we saw a police officer standing on a street corner, and he directed us to the hotel.
B. . . . we were all ready to take a walk, but not quite like the one I was about to take . . .
C. We ran for a while because I did not want to be late, especially since I was . . .
D. When we could see the hotel down the road, we said good-bye . . .

Total Problems:	Total Correct:	Score:

Read the passage. Circle the letter beside each correct answer.

A Bottle of Perfume

Jason Perkins had been a problem student since he set foot into Mrs. Harris's sixth-grade class. Every day he came into class poorly dressed, unclean, and inattentive. Whenever Mrs. Harris marked his paper "unsatisfactory," she thought to herself, "Why is this student wasting my time?"

Soon the Christmas season was approaching, and Mrs. Harris was giving her usual reviews. When she came upon Jason's review, she noticed that other teachers had reviewed him as being "very bright and a joy to have around." Confused, Mrs. Harris looked further into the matter and discovered that Jason had been reared by just his mother until this past summer. However, during the summer, she had passed away and custody had been given to his father who was not interested in raising a child. Mrs. Harris felt badly for not understanding and being more sympathetic.

The day before Christmas vacation, Mrs. Harris opened the presents that the children had brought her. All the presents were neatly wrapped except for Jason's, which was sloppily wrapped in newspaper. As she opened Jason's present, she discovered it was an almost empty bottle of perfume. Being courteous, Mrs. Harris smiled and thanked Jason and sprayed a little perfume on herself. As the children were leaving for Christmas vacation, Jason stopped at her desk and said, "You know, Mrs. Harris, today you smell just like my mother." As Jason walked out of the classroom, Mrs. Harris began to cry.

1. What conclusion had Mrs. Harris drawn before discovering the truth about Jason?

A. Jason was a poor student who didn't care about school.

B. Because Jason was unclean, inattentive, and poorly dressed, he was not capable of being intelligent and a fun student with whom to work.

C. Jason's other teachers must have made a mistake in reviewing him.

D. Jason should have been kept in the fifth grade.

2. What conclusion can the reader make after reading the story?

A. Mrs. Harris will continue to wonder why Jason is wasting her time in class.

B. Jason will continue to make unsatisfactory marks in Mrs. Harris's class.

C. Mrs. Harris will become more attentive and helpful to Jason.

D. Jason will quit school and run away from his father.

Total Problems: **Total Correct:** **Score:**

Name ______________________________

Read the passage. Circle the letter beside the correct answer.

The Red Path

One lazy Sunday afternoon, two friends, Randy and Lynn, decided to go hiking at the local state park. The weather was mild and beautiful, so they knew it would be a good day to spend outdoors. After quickly packing a picnic lunch, Randy and Lynn were on their way.

When they arrived, they chose one of the numerous paths available. Each path was marked by different colors of spray paint that marked the trees and plants in the path. It looked as if it would be impossible to get lost, or so they thought.

The path they chose was marked with red paint. Following the path for about fifteen minutes, Randy and Lynn became hungry and decided to stop and eat the picnic lunch. This quickly replenished their energy, and they were ready to continue the hike. As they walked, they enjoyed the majestic mountains, falling leaves, and the bubbling creek. It was a beautiful day, and it did not seem that anything could go wrong. However, as they were enjoying the surrounding nature, they had accidentally wandered onto the orange path.

Feeling that orange would meet back with the red path, they continued on the path. Soon, the orange led to yellow, and Randy and Lynn realized they had no idea where they were going. Eventually, they found signs pointing in opposite directions, so they chose one and hoped for the best. After walking for about two hours, they began to think their beautiful scenery had turned into a horrible prison from which there seemed to be no escape. It would soon be dark and difficult to see the paint colors, so they knew they had to walk fast.

Just when sheer panic and hopelessness were about to take hold, Randy noticed that things were starting to look familiar. All this time, they had just been going in a big circle! There had been no cause for distress; they were not lost after all. After coming to this joyous realization, it took them only about five minutes to find their way back to the car. Randy and Lynn decided it would be awhile before they went hiking again.

1. After reading the above passage, what conclusion can you draw?

A. Hiking in a state park can be fun if the weather is mild.
B. A person should never hike alone.
C. When hiking in the woods, pay constant attention to where you are going to prevent getting lost.
D. Always hike on the red path when you hike in a state park.

Total Problems:	**Total Correct:**	**Score:**

Name ______________________________

Read the passage and answer the questions on the following page.

Flitter the Butterfly

Flitter the butterfly was courageous, soaring through the Texas skies all day and night. Sweeping through the big **cumulus** clouds, Flitter never stopped to think about what might lie ahead of her. The other insects, especially George the grasshopper, tried to warn her of the **predators** that might leap at her when she was not paying attention, but Flitter wouldn't bother to listen. She wanted to be adventurous, and she thought the other insects were envious of her.

Besides thinking Flitter was courageous, the insects also thought she had lost her little mind. Flitter was still young and didn't know what other species there were out in the world. However, the insects realized that Flitter would find out eventually, and hoped she would survive.

One day when Flitter was out enjoying her morning flight, she came upon a bird's nest high in a maple tree. Immediately, she flew down into the nest that was occupied by four little birds. Thinking Flitter was their mother, they began snapping their little beaks. Flitter thought they were playing with her, so she began to tease them by swooping down and then flying up into the air. In fact, she was having so much fun she didn't realize what was happening behind her back. Berta, the mother bird, was swooping down intending to use Flitter as the babies' meal.

Flitter looked up just in time to move out of the way of Berta's sharp beak. Flitter started flapping her wings as fast as she could to get away, but immediately Berta gave chase to her. Flitter dove into a tree and into a little hole in the tree trunk. Realizing Flitter had gotten away, Berta returned to her babies.

Slowly, Flitter came out of the hole in the tree trunk and then flew as fast as she could back to her home to find all the other insects waiting on her. Sharing her story with everyone, Flitter appeared to have learned an important lesson that day. Although the insects told Flitter they had been trying to warn her about all the predators, they were still thankful and proud that Flitter had survived that day.

Read each question. Circle the letter beside each correct answer.

1. With whom does Flitter have a dangerous encounter one day on her morning flight?
   A. George
   B. Texas
   C. Berta
   D. baby birds

2. Which one of the following words best describes Flitter?
   A. selfish
   B. clown
   C. smart
   D. courageous

3. When Flitter escaped her predator, where did she hide?
   A. hole in the ground
   B. hole in the tree trunk
   C. hole in the cumulus clouds
   D. hole in the building

4. "Flitter the Butterfly" is a story about:
   A. a young insect who learns an important lesson about predators
   B. a nest of baby birds
   C. a group of insects who live and work together
   D. a young boy who learns how to survive in the world

5. Another word for "predator" is:
   A. Berta
   B. an animal that chirps
   C. a preying animal
   D. insect

6. How many baby birds were found in the nest?
   A. 3
   B. 4
   C. 10
   D. 1

7. George, a friend of Flitter, is a:
   A. grasshopper
   B. snail
   C. bird
   D. bug

8. If you are "envious" of someone, you are:
   A. disliked
   B. loved
   C. jealous
   D. loathed

Total Problems: Total Correct: Score:

Name ____________________

Figurative Language uses devices such as similes, metaphors, personification, and alliteration.
Example: *The girl is beautiful.* (Literal Language)
The girl is like a rose. (Figurative Language)

Read the poems and circle the letter beside each correct answer.

Two Worlds

Between me and the sunset,
every twig jumping out of the blazing orange
like a guardian standing at the portal
between two opposite worlds.
This world has grown familiar;
I am accustomed to its gristmill rhythm.
The other is wild and untamed.
It hasn't learned to be subdued,
forced into ill-fitting fetters.
Wonders lie hidden in the glowing orange,
but is there danger too?

1. In the third line, "like a guardian," is what figure of speech?
- A. metaphor
- B. simile
- C. irony
- D. pun

2. Read lines 7-9, " The other . . . fetters." What is the poet saying about the other world?
- A. It has become too familiar and tame.
- B. It is between the sun and the moon.
- C. It hasn't become routine and tamed.
- D. It is rhythmical with twigs jumping in the sun.

Frosty

The snowman came last night
and filled the sky with shadows
and covered the ground with white.
He did his job with no mistake,
as he carefully made each snowflake.
And every field that he had chosen
will surely be found frozen.
I watched the snow throughout the day
knowing his gift would not stay
since the sun will come out to melt it away.

3. Why won't the snow stay?
- A. The snowman will take it with him.
- B. The rain is going to dissolve it.
- C. The fields don't like it.
- D. The sun will melt it.

4. Who is the "he" referring to in line 4?
- A. night
- B. snowflake
- C. snowman
- D. sky

Total Problems: Total Correct: Score:

Read the poem and circle the letter beside each correct answer.

An Apple Tree

I have an apple tree
in my garden,
but the apples do not fall
until they are rotten.

They hit the steadfast ground
and burst apart,
seeds floating in the apple
sauce like ships out of port.

Small vessels sailing down
into the soil,
hoping to establish their
colonies on the shore.

The towns will be trees
mirroring life
in the form of rotten fruit
bursting in my garden.

1. In the second stanza, "seeds floating in the apple sauce like ships out of port," what is the dominant figure of speech?

A. metaphor
B. pun
C. simile
D. personification

2. In the third stanza, what are the "Small vessels"?

A. ships
B. seeds
C. trees
D. fruit

3. "Small vessels," in the third stanza, is a figure of speech known as a:

A. simile
B. paradox
C. personification
D. metaphor

4. Referring to the third stanza: What are the "vessels" hoping to accomplish?

A. The ships, with people on board, are hoping to establish a new colony.
B. The ships are carrying people to Australia—the down under.
C. The apple seeds fall into the soil hoping to germinate to produce apple trees.
D. The little ships are sinking into the quick soil.

Total Problems: **Total Correct:** **Score:**

Name ________________________________

Read the passage. As you consider the meanings of the words in bold, pay close attention to the other words (clues) that surround the bold words. Choose a word from the word box to replace each bold word and write it in the blank provided.

The Life of a Soda Bottle

When I was born, my mother never held me, except for when she shook me to see if my head was on straight. If my head wasn't on straight, she said that I would be considered flat and no one would want me.

My machine mother filled me with a sweet, bubbly liquid. But this was for others to enjoy—not me. She taught me about the world outside our little factory. My father told me that the world was very **merciless** and to be careful once I was on my own.

One day I left my safe home and my machine-like parents, and **ventured** into the "cruel" world. I even left my big, **spacious** room to be packed tightly together for a long, long journey.

When we finally reached our **destination**, I started my new life. I had a new home and made some new friends, some whom had traveled with me from my own home. However, one afternoon a lady came along and with one press of a button, I was out of house and home. She was cruel to me.

My dad had said it would be like this. I **presume** I never believed him. The lady twisted my head off and **regenerated** herself with all my insides. Then, when she was finished, there was nothing more left of me. My life was over.

1. presume ____________________
2. merciless ____________________
3. ventured ____________________
4. regenerated ____________________
5. destination ____________________
6. spacious ____________________

Word Box
- cruel
- guess
- location
- roomy
- traveled
- refreshed

Total Problems: Total Correct: Score:

Read the passage and answer the questions on pages 24-25.

Best Friends

Hannah Roberts has been my best friend since kindergarten. We have been through many experiences together: slumber parties, football games, cheerleading tryouts, and braces. We have watched one another grow into intelligent, witty, and beautiful young women. I consider myself lucky to have her as my best friend.

In the tenth grade we experienced one of our most important milestones together: our sixteenth birthdays! My sixteenth didn't come until six months after Hannah's. Hannah's sixteenth birthday party was a blast. Her parents surprised her with a car—not a new one, but one that looked almost new. Immediately, she began describing all the places we would go and all the things we could do, now that she had a car. I was just as excited as she was, thinking of all the fun we would have together. It didn't take long for Hannah to get her driver's license. Although my parents were reluctant to let me ride with Hannah alone, eventually they gave in and decided it would be all right.

Our first long-distance driving trip was to the mall, only twenty-five miles from our small town of Manchester, a route I could easily trace in my sleep. That night as I waited for Hannah to pick me up, I began to feel incredibly independent. My parents were finally trusting me, and it felt good. Of course, when Hannah arrived, they still did what I expected, lecturing us on car safety, traffic signals, passing other cars, and intoxicated drivers.

Hannah's driving was safe, and she obeyed all the traffic laws, never attempting to speed or show off. On the way, we discussed our dreams and goals and how we were growing up. She seemed to be so sentimental as we drove along.

After shopping for a long time at the mall, we ate dinner at an Italian restaurant and headed home. It was later than we thought, so we called our parents from my cellular phone to let them know we were safe. We were about five miles from home when a car pulled out in front of us. Hannah pressed hard on the brakes with her foot, but we were too close. We slammed into the side of the car.

The next thing I remember is waking up with a bandaged arm in Rockford emergency room. In the same room lay a man with injuries to the head and arm. I had no sense of what was going on, and looking around, I noticed that Hannah was not in the room. A nurse, a couple of feet away from me, noticed I was awake and called my parents. The three of them were beside me almost immediately. They explained to me that Hannah was hurt very badly. The doctors said she would heal eventually, but it was going to take a long time.

Many months have passed since that horrific night. Hannah is progressing slowly. I visit her every day after school to bolster her spirits and help her catch up with schoolwork. Although the car accident was tragic, Hannah and I have grown closer. I got my driver's license today. I cannot wait for Hannah to get well so that I can drive her to the mall.

Name ______________________________________

Read each question. Circle the letter beside the correct answer where appropriate.

1. The story is mainly about:
   - A. two best friends that get in a car accident
   - B. getting braces
   - C. driving a car on your own for the first time
   - D. learning to accept yourself

2. Number the sentences in the order in which they occurred in the story.

____ The girls ate at an Italian restaurant.
____ Hannah turned sixteen.
____ The narrator visited Hannah every day after school.
____ The narrator got her driver's license.
____ The narrator woke up in the emergency room.
____ The girls drove to the mall.

3. "Many months have passed since that horrific night." In this sentence from the story, "horrific" means:
   - A. wonderful
   - B. memorable
   - C. stormy
   - D. horrible

4. Someone who is laughing "hysterically" is someone who:
   - A. has a medical problem
   - B. is laughing uncontrollably
   - C. has permanent hiccups
   - D. makes fun of people who laugh

5. In what town do the girls live?
   - A. Manchester
   - B. Chattanooga
   - C. Rockford
   - D. New York

Total Problems: Total Correct: Score:

Name ______________________________

Read each question. Circle the letter beside each correct answer.

6. According to the passage, the girls experienced all of the following together except:
  A. going to college
  B. turning sixteen
  C. cheerleading tryouts
  D. braces

7. Which of the following words is a synonym for "milestone"?
  A. granite
  B. speedometer
  C. brick
  D. benchmark

8. Which of the following is false?
  A. The girls called their parents to tell them they would be late.
  B. The girls had been friends since kindergarten.
  C. The girls ate dinner at an Italian restaurant.
  D. Hannah drove recklessly to the mall.

9. What did Hannah receive from her parents for her birthday?
  A. a computer
  B. a car
  C. a camera
  D. concert tickets

10. Why might the narrator's parents have lectured the girls on driving safely?
  A. They didn't want the girls to have any fun.
  B. They thought Hannah's car had faulty brakes.
  C. Hannah was a new driver.
  D. They were cruel and liked to yell.

11. Who was in the emergency room when the narrator awoke?
  A. Hannah, the nurse, and Hannah's parents
  B. the narrator's parents, an injured man, and the nurse
  C. Hannah and an injured man
  D. Hannah's parents, the narrator's parents, and the nurse

Total Problems: **Total Correct:** **Score:**

Read the passage. Answer the questions on the following page.

Margaret Farquar

I'm the kind of guy who can't hurt other people's feelings. I guess I just cannot stand to see someone else hurt because of what I do or say.

When I was fourteen, there was a girl, Margaret Farquar, who really liked me. In middle school, when someone liked you it was taken as a compliment. To put things into a better **perspective**, allow me to take you back to McNeil Middle School, just two years ago.

"Hey Chris," I shouted as my best friend came walking down the hall toward me. Chris was tall and lanky, and his long, shaggy, brown hair accented his pale blue eyes.

"Look," he started, "my mom can't take me to work after school, and. . ." I cut him off before he could finish because I knew what he wanted.

"Sure, my mom can give you a ride, but be here right after school because last time we waited on you for half an hour."

"All right. I'll hurry," he almost yelled. Chris told me about this girl in his Spanish class who really liked me.

Excitedly, I asked, "Who?"

"Margaret Farquar," he said, almost in a whisper. The words seemed to come out **languidly** and painfully as my stomach sank to the floor. I asked Chris to repeat the name. Yes, he had said it: Margaret Farquar.

"She said that she was hoping you would ask her to the Valentine dance. If I were you, I would keep my distance. Do you have any idea what this could do to your reputation?"

Still in complete shock, I replied, "Yeah, I know. I'm going to dash to the bathroom. The bell is about to ring. Don't forget to be here after school because at 2:40 I'm leaving."

I quickly walked away, hoping no one had heard the conversation. As I rounded the corner to the bathroom, it happened. "Nathan," somebody shouted, but the 'th' in my name sounded contorted and twisted. Slowly, I turned around to see Margaret, grinning with all her teeth showing. "How's it going?" she said, with her full attention focused on me, only me.

"Hi, Margaret," I said almost inaudibly, while at the same time looking over my shoulder to make sure nobody was watching.

"Look, I don't have a date for the dance, and I was wondering if you didn't ...." There was a pause.

"Well, you see, I already have a date," I replied, hoping she didn't know I really didn't have one. But she did.

"Really? Yesterday Chris told me that you weren't going with anyone."

"Here's the thing. I am planning to ask someone," I replied. This really wasn't a lie; I just didn't yet know whom I was going to ask.

"Oh? Well...," she didn't finish her sentence before tears formed in the corners of her eyes.

Just then the bell rang. She turned and slowly walked away, and I just stood there, thinking and thinking. I began to admire her courage and feel ashamed of my own cowardly lie. It was then, at that moment, that something overcame me. I called her name, loudly this time, and I have never regretted it.

Name ______________________________ **Margaret Farquar**

Read each question. Circle the letter beside each correct answer.

1. Referring to: "The words seemed to come out languidly,"—the word "languidly" means:
   - A. slowly
   - B. quickly
   - C. lively
   - D. briskly

2. The main idea of the story is that:
   - A. High school is a stressful time for all teenagers.
   - B. No one should be made to feel humiliated because of who he is.
   - C. The Valentine dance is a big event, but not everyone is able to attend.
   - D. Friends cannot always be trusted.

3. In the last paragraph, the narrator says "something overcame me." What inference is implied here, based on reading the entire story?
   - A. Margaret should not have approached him so aggressively.
   - B. The narrator should have listened more closely to Chris's advice.
   - C. The narrator realized that he should not ask Margaret to the dance.
   - D. The narrator feels badly that he is "responsible" for Margaret's tears and sadness.

4. All the following describe Chris except:
   - A. pale blue eyes
   - B. tall and lanky
   - C. short, blond hair
   - D. best friend

5. Which one of the following statements is false?
   - A. The name of the school is McNeil Middle School.
   - B. The narrator was fifteen when Margaret liked him.
   - C. The name of the narrator is Nathan.
   - D. Margaret was in Chris's Spanish class.

Total Problems: **Total Correct:** **Score:**

Read the passage and answer the questions on the following page.

The Corn Patch Ghost

There is a true story that my grandmother tells, and whenever she tells it, everyone has a good laugh, everyone except my great-grandfather. The story takes place a long time ago, back in the early 1900s in a rural area.

It was the second time that month that he had been out way past dark. The kids were distressed, especially Shirley, who repeated "Daddy is still not home, Mama." Shirley was the most **fervent** of the six children, and she loved Daddy very much.

"Don't you worry, Shirley. I'll make sure he will be home tomorrow night," Mama guaranteed. From the look on Mama's face, we could tell she was up to something. We would just have to wait and see.

As we sat down for supper, each in his or her own place, my oldest brother asked if he should ask the blessing. "Go ahead, son," said Mama, eyeing the empty seat directly across from hers.

After supper I helped to put the two young babies to bed and started on my schoolwork, while Henry and Agnes washed the dishes and cleaned the kitchen. "Where is Mama?" I asked my older sister Lee.

"Well, I don't know," replied Lee, "Maybe she went to the barn."

I was a little baffled; it wasn't like Mama to leave the house after dark, but on the other hand, she was not the type to explain herself to anyone. I finished my schoolwork, prepared for bed, and read a bedtime story to Tina, my younger sister who had just begun school this year.

"I hope Mama is safe," I said nervously to Lee before retiring to bed.

"I'm almost positive she is just fine," Lee said half assuringly. She didn't sound too sure of herself, but she was trying to be the grown-up in the house. Then, she rushed the rest of us off to bed. Lee and I shared a bed, and I was exceptionally glad that night.

"I hope Mama gets back soon," I said worriedly as Lee and I hid under the covers. "It is really chilly out." Lee just nodded her head, and I began to drift into a fitful sleep when a scream roused me out of bed. Quickly, Lee and I ran to the window to get a look at the disturbance outside. Just as I raised the window shade, the front door burst open and Daddy, out of breath and white as a sheet, entered the house. By then, Lee and I were in the front room witnessing my daddy's state of being. Lee yelled, "What's going on?"

"Ghost!" he tried to whisper. "A ghost in the corn patch! It chased me all the way to the house!" He certainly looked as if he had seen a ghost, but it didn't take Lee and me long to realize that Daddy had again stopped at Uncle Fred's for a little swig of moonshine. "Quick, girls, get into bed, and don't make a sound," he instructed us. We did as he said, and shortly thereafter we heard the front door open again. We began to piece together the puzzle and had a great laugh.

Early the next morning, Mama was there to get all of us out of bed. As Lee and I were warming by the fire, Mama winked and pulled a white sheet from under the couch as she casually told us that Daddy would not be missing any more suppers for awhile. Then, Lee said, "I guess Daddy really did see a ghost."

Read each question. Circle the letter beside each correct answer.

1. Referring to the last paragraph when Mama "winked and pulled a white sheet from under the couch," one might possibly conclude that:
   A. Mama had hidden Daddy's favorite white sheet under the couch.
   B. Mama was planning to do something with the white sheet.
   C. Mama was the ghost in the corn patch that scared Daddy.
   D. Mama was planning to give Daddy a new white sheet.

2. A synonym for the word "fervent" is:
   A. impassioned
   B. sleepy
   C. smart
   D. athletic

3. In the tenth paragraph, what are the context clues for the meaning of the word "roused"?
   A. fitful sleep
   B. awakened
   C. drift
   D. began

4. All of the following are true except:
   A. Tina had just begun school.
   B. Lee and the narrator shared a bed for sleeping.
   C. Daddy had been at Uncle Frankie's drinking moonshine.
   D. Shirley was the emotional child in the family.

Total Problems: **Total Correct:** **Score:**

Read the passage and answer the questions on the following page.

Losing Touch

The farm was ready for slumber, and he could finally sit down and think. He desperately needed to think. Lately, he was having so much trouble trying to remember. Settling into his worn chair, he gazed out the window and slipped into a deep meditation. He owned a farm. He had a wife. He called her Darling.

Darling...where was she? Oh, yes, there she was in the kitchen preparing a meal. He could hear her. He had three sons and a daughter. And where were they? He glanced at the clock. They should have been home from school hours ago. He became agitated as he listened for their childish voices to penetrate the fog covering his mind. No...nothing.

He slowly rose and walked into the kitchen. He asked Darling where the children were. She turned to him with her sweet smile, but the smile quickly faded when she noticed he wasn't jesting. She quietly explained to him that the children were grown now and had families of their own. Puzzled, he sat down. Yes, this was true. He remembered now; Darling had told him this yesterday. He smiled at her before pulling her into his arms.

"I love you, Darling. I promise I will never forget you," he told her. A tear slipped from her big green eyes, and he kissed it away. She smiled then and they sat down to dinner. He had been so nervous lately. Later, they went into the living room where he got out their picture albums and requested that she go over the pictures with him, just so he wouldn't forget. As he looked at the pictures, **immersed** in naming all the people in the pictures and the places they had traveled, she looked at him sadly. She nodded as he repeated every name correctly. Gently, she took his hand. He was slipping from her every day, though he struggled against it. She knew not how, only that he was slowly losing touch with their perfect world. Once, when he glanced up and grinned at her, she was lost in his deep blue eyes.

The days and nights became repetitious. He found it too difficult sometimes. He was awakened suddenly from his slumber. Wiping the sweat from his brow, he crept from their bed, careful not to awaken Darling. He needed to think. He walked to the window and gazed at the orange moon. He owned a farm. He had a wife. He called her Darling. He had three sons and a daughter. Where were they? Oh, yes...with their families. He sighed in relief. He remembered. He was fine.

Many nights he awoke, frantic to remember. He paced around the room straining to remember. There was his farm, his Darling, his sons, and a daughter.

"What is wrong?" Darling would ask him.

"I'm just nervous, Darling, go back to sleep."

One evening as she called him to supper the third time, she knew something was wrong. She found him at his desk. Walking quietly behind him, she saw he was desperately writing the names of his family. As she turned and silently left the room, tears streamed down her face, and she knew he was going to leave her. His mind was becoming too cluttered to remember.

Read each question. Circle the letter beside each correct answer.

1. One might conclude that since the old man is having trouble remembering events and people, he might be experiencing the symptoms of:
   A. cancer
   B. tuberculosis
   C. Alzheimer's
   D. malaria

2. In the fourth paragraph, what is another word that means "immersed"?
   A. daydreamed
   B. absorbed
   C. unabsorbed
   D. fantasized

3. Which one of the following is not true about the man's family?
   A. The children are grown and have families of their own.
   B. He lives on a farm with Darling, his wife.
   C. Sometimes he remembered events, and sometimes he did not.
   D. He had two sons and a daughter.

4. "The days and nights became repetitious. He found it too difficult sometimes. He was awakened suddenly from his slumber." What are the context clues for the meaning of "slumber"?
   A. became repetitious
   B. days and nights
   C. awakened from
   D. too difficult

5. Referring to the fourth paragraph and the sentence, "Once, when he glanced up and grinned at her, she was lost in his deep blue eyes," one could infer that:
   A. She is still very much in love with her husband.
   B. She is trying to analyze and assess her husband's illness.
   C. She has the same illness as he.
   D. She was confused by what he was saying and doing.

Total Problems: **Total Correct:** **Score:**

Read the passage and answer the questions on the following page.

Mallory's Big Splash

Summer is a favorite time of the year for my family. For me, summer means rest and relaxation from the busy school year. For Mallory and Trey, my younger sister and brother, summer means independence. The three of us have grown up on a farm, which has instilled in us a strong sense of independence. During the summer, Mallory and Trey are able to come and go as they please, as long as they do not wander off the farm and get into any trouble.

A few summers ago on a typical hot July day, Mallory and Trey were carelessly riding their bicycles and sporting about in the pasture. Feeling restless, they decided to race their bikes down to the pond to catch frogs, bugs, and snakes. Mallory was in the lead, but Trey was close behind. As Mallory approached the pond, a swarm of gnats overcame her and temporarily blinded her. With her bike still moving and her eyes closed, she sailed off the **embankment** that surrounded the pond, and into the murky water with a big splash.

Trey arrived at the pond a few seconds later. He recounts a scene he will never forget. Mallory was standing up to her waist in muddy water with green pond algae limply hanging from her head and arms. Instead of immediately going to her rescue, Trey just stood there gawking and teasing her as some bratty little brothers would. Furthermore, he quickly ran home to share Mallory's **humiliation** with Mom. He just knew, and hoped, that Mallory would get into trouble for not watching where she was going.

As Trey was trying to explain to Mom what had happened, Mallory, dripping wet with green algae all over her body, knocked on the back door. When Mom went to the door, all she could do was laugh and laugh. Mom later said that Mallory looked like a little swamp monster from some movie, and she didn't smell too good either.

Trey had hoped Mallory would receive some kind of punishment because he was that type of brother. Mom thought Mallory's ordeal was punishment enough, and so did I. However, to this day our family still has a big laugh whenever the story of Mallory's big splash is retold.

Name ______________________________

Read each question. Circle the letter beside each correct answer.

1. What caused Mallory to plunge into the murky pond?
   A. She was not watching very closely as she rode her bike.
   B. Trey purposely pushed her into the water.
   C. A swarm of gnats overcame her and temporarily blinded her.
   D. She was trying to get away from a raging bull.

2. An antonym for the word "humiliation" is:
   A. anger
   B. praise
   C. downgrading
   D. embarrassment

3. Which one of the following events happened first?
   A. Mallory, dripping wet with green algae all over her body, knocked on the door.
   B. He quickly ran home to share Mallory's humiliation with Mom.
   C. They decided to race their bikes down to the pond to catch frogs, bugs, and snakes.
   D. She sailed off the embankment that surrounded the pond, and into the murky water.

4. Referring to the following sentences taken from the third paragraph, "Trey arrived at the pond a few seconds later. He recounts a scene he will never forget,"—what are the context clues for the word "recounts"?
   A. at the pond
   B. never forget
   C. a scene
   D. a few seconds later

5. When Mother saw Mallory standing in the doorway, she said Mallory looked like:
   A. a frog
   B. brown, murky water
   C. green algae
   D. a little swamp monster

6. What is the setting of the story?
   A. a school
   B. a bank
   C. a farm
   D. a kitchen

7. Referring to the phrase, "she sailed off the embankment,"—"embankment" means a:
   A. slope
   B. straight road
   C. river
   D. narrow bridge

Total Problems:	Total Correct:	Score:

Read the passage and answer the questions on the following page.

The Parachute

Bruner Ray Fortenberry is such a wonderful name for a cat. At least, I think so. Bruner was such a fun cat, and he brought many good times and memories to my family and me. Playful and **nimble**, Bruner loved to hide and tangle with boxes. My Aunt Sammi always enjoyed spinning him in a box until he would jump out and lay crouched on the floor as if he were stalking the box. He would remain in this position until something else diverted his attention. He could go on like this for hours at a time, as long as someone was willing to play with him.

Bruner also loved to play with paper bags. During Christmas vacation one year, Bruner was playing in a grocery bag while I was emptying the trash. As I was putting a new trash bag into the can, I realized that Bruner had just about had a heart attack. He really hated the sound of trash bags. In fact, this startled him so badly that he shot out of the kitchen like lightning. However, somehow during his great endeavor to get away, he managed to wrap a grocery bag around his neck and stomach. At that moment, all I could think about was the Christmas tree. I was just hoping that he would not destroy the tree while trying to get out of what he thought was harm's way.

Considering Bruner was running as fast as a bullet, I could not see how he could possibly miss the tree. Contrary to my beliefs, he managed to dodge the tree, but he did run directly into the piano. This scene happened so quickly I did not know how to react. He seemed so pitiful and awestruck that I just wanted to hold him. Even though he was still wrapped in the grocery bag, he appeared to be okay because he was still jumping and trying to untangle himself. When I realized he was not hurt, I began laughing. Replaying the scene in my mind, I sat on the floor and laughed. This jocund cat! Again, Bruner became startled, and he took off running just as he did the first time. That was when I realized that the bag on his back looked like a parachute.

Bruner recently became very sick and had to be put to sleep. Sometimes, I think about him and feel sad, but then I think about his "parachute" incident and laugh. Even though he is not with me anymore, he left me with some lasting memories.

Name ______________________________

Read each question. Circle the letter beside each correct answer.

1. "Playful and *nimble*, Bruner loved to hide and tangle with boxes." "Nimble" means:
   A. quick
   B. funny
   C. easy
   D. afraid

2. The main idea is:
   A. Don't allow your pet to play with cardboard boxes.
   B. Pets can be clumsy and hazardous if allowed to play in the house.
   C. Be careful when you permit pets near Christmas trees.
   D. Pets can provide happy memories.

3. Which one of the following events happened last in the story?
   A. He appeared to be okay because he was still jumping and trying to untangle himself.
   B. Bruner was playing in a grocery bag while I was emptying the trash.
   C. He managed to wrap a grocery bag. . .around his neck and stomach.
   D. My Aunt Sammi always enjoyed spinning him in a box.

4. Read the fourth paragraph and especially the following sentence: "When I realized he was not hurt, I began laughing. Replaying the scene in my mind, I sat on the floor and laughed. This jocund cat!" What is a context clue for the word "jocund"?
   A. replaying
   B. lay
   C. laughed
   D. hurt

5. Where does the title of the story originate?
   A. Wearing a parachute once, Bruner jumped out of a plane.
   B. Bruner looked like he was wearing a parachute when he was running with a bag wrapped around him.
   C. Bruner is big and round as a parachute.
   D. Bruner became entangled in a parachute and could not see where he was running.

Total Problems: **Total Correct:** **Score:**

Read the passage and answer the questions on the following page.

The Lunar Danger

The view from the Fifth Lunar Observatory was breathtaking. The stars shine brighter there than on Earth. Without a true atmosphere, the Earth's moon is a great location for a celestial observatory. My name is Michael, and I worked aboard the observatory, built in 2112, located just south of the Tsiolkovsky Crater. This was an ideal location because most of the time the main telescope faced away from the sun. We enjoyed an **unobstructed** view of the heavens but the spacecraft had to shield us from temperatures nearing –200°F.

My usual workday consisted of maneuvering the main telescope, Hubble IV, which was the descendent of the original Hubble telescope. I had an assistant, Robert, to help me. Every morning we received coordinates of a star, constellation, or planet that interested scientists on Earth.

On November 7, 2113, Robert and I received orders to focus the telescope on the constellation Gemini. According to the report we received, scientists had picked up electromagnetic activity near Gemini. Robert and I began entering the data into the computer and focusing the telescope. As the Hubble IV was rotating in the direction of Gemini, the main motor started smoking. I yelled at Robert to turn off the machine. By the time he pressed the last button, the main observation room had filled with smoke. That was the least of our problems; the electrical fire had also knocked out our main power.

Luckily, the emergency lights came on, but our temperature control unit was severely damaged. Without the TCU, a stable temperature of 72°F could not be maintained in the lunar complex. I estimated we had only ninety minutes before we would freeze.

Robert reminded me of an escape rover in one of the cargo bays. Where would we go, though? The nearest settlement was the Fourth Lunar Observatory, but it had been closed for six years. Our situation worsened by the minute. I watched the temperature on the thermometer drop every minute. We couldn't contact anyone since we were on the far side of the moon. The temperature was down to 54°, and I was feeling sick. This looked like the end.

As I was trying to keep warm, I glanced at Robert's watch. It was then 4:05 P.M. Suddenly, I was overwhelmed with joy. The lunar sunrise was to take place at 4:08 P.M. With the sun's rays shining directly on us, we would begin to warm. Although the outside temperature could reach 250°F, we would have plenty of time to start the cooling system manually. Using the outside solar panels for energy, we successfully started the cooling system.

However, our troubles were not over yet. Soon the sun would go down, and we would surely freeze to death. However, we were able to contact the new international space station and request that Earth send down a rescue ship and pick us up. On our way home, I began to look forward to the relatively stable temperatures of planet Earth.

Name ______________________________

Read each question. Circle the letter beside each correct answer.

1. Who rescued Robert and the narrator?
- A. Gemini voyager
- B. Sixth Lunar Observatory
- C. Challenger
- D. people from the international space station

2. An inference one could make after reading the story is that:
- A. Electromagnetic activity should be studied more closely.
- B. Life outside Earth is difficult to maintain.
- C. Human beings should not attempt to live outside of Earth.
- D. There are some planets near Earth with human life.

3. What was the cause of the accident that eventually sent Robert and the narrator home to Earth?
- A. attack from Gemini
- B. lightning storm
- C. electrical fire
- D. electromagnetic activity

4. A word that means the opposite of "unobstructed" is:
- A. non-interference
- B. unimpede
- C. blocked
- D. view

5. The temperature outside the observatory could reach as high as:
- A. 200°F
- B. 250°F
- C. –250°F
- D. 72°F

Total Problems: **Total Correct:** **Score:**

Read the passage and answer the questions on the following page.

Sweet Sixteen

Staying with a friend while my mother and stepfather were out of town, I woke up at a strange house with one of those familiar bad feelings in my stomach. I was sixteen today, but that didn't mean much to me for some reason.

Recently, I had decided to leave my mother to live with my father and stepmother in Alabama because my stepfather and I got along as well as the coyote and the roadrunner. Perhaps this is a bit of an overstatement concerning our relationship, but still, I was moving.

After breakfast, Jackie convinced me that I should visit our other friend, Kate. She had a big swimming pool, but today swimming didn't seem so exciting. To make Jackie and Kate happy, I decided to oblige and visit Kate. However, this feeling in my stomach had been tenacious since the day I decided to leave and live with my father in Alabama. But today, for my friends, I tried to look as if I were enjoying myself.

After a long drive, we finally pulled into Kate's driveway. When I knocked on the door, Kate answered and immediately ordered me to shut my eyes because she had a surprise for me. As Kate led me around the yard, I imagined a birthday present that I probably would hate but would have to pretend to like.

After a few minutes of sensing that we were walking around the house to the back, Kate finally allowed me to open my eyes. I was facing the swimming pool, and every person I had cared about at all since the day I moved to Atlanta was there at the pool, yelling "Surprise!" For a split second, I did not quite know how to react or what to say, and it felt like my heart stopped beating for a few seconds.

That day took away the dire feeling in my stomach, and I have never had that feeling again. The realization that even after I moved away my friends would still be there for me made me a stronger person. I was strong enough after that day to leave and begin a new life because I knew that no matter what happened, my friends would always be there for me.

My sweet sixteen birthday turned out to be the best birthday yet, and the new friends I have made here in Alabama will undoubtedly make my next birthday even better.

Read each question. Circle the letter beside each correct answer.

1. The story is mainly about:
   A. a swimming party
   B. friendship
   C. an unfair stepfather
   D. a sixteenth birthday

2. Referring to: "However, this feeling in my stomach had been tenacious since the day I decided to leave and live with my father in Alabama,"—the context clues for the meaning of the word "tenacious" are:
   A. in my stomach
   B. to leave and live
   C. I decided
   D. feeling in my stomach

3. Which one of the following statements is not true?
   A. Kate answered and immediately ordered me to shut my eyes because she had a surprise for me.
   B. She convinced me that I should visit our other friend Kate.
   C. Every person I cared about at all since the day I moved to Alabama was there.
   D. I had decided to leave my mother to live with my father and stepmother.

4. A synonym for the word "dire" is:
   A. nauseous
   B. empty
   C. horrible
   D. guilty

5. Which of the following statements is a conclusion one might draw from reading the story?
   A. Life is easier if one has good friends on whom to depend.
   B. One should accept a stepparent, regardless of differences of opinion.
   C. Birthday parties for sixteen-year-olds are the best in Atlanta.
   D. Don't count on your friends to be there when you need them.

Total Problems:	Total Correct:	Score:

Read the passage and answer the questions on the following page.

Refuse Fear

During the summer between my eighth- and ninth-grade years, I went to Maui, Hawaii, on a vacation with my family. Since I had never been to Hawaii, I decided I wanted to do all I could to enjoy myself. There were many exciting activities, including scuba diving, biking, surfing, and parasailing. Since I tended to be afraid of heights and deep water, I decided to engage in parasailing in order to overcome this fear.

When we arrived at the beach, our coordinator told us that the boat was malfunctioning, so we would have to wait until another boat was ready. This waiting did not help my nerves one bit. I kept thinking this was a sign for me to back out. I tried to calm my nerves by swimming and playing on the beach with my sister.

The wait was only about one hour, and then we were on our way. The little motor-powered raft transported us to the main boat sitting out in the water. I thought my nerves had calmed until I stepped onto the main boat, and then I almost panicked. I said to my family that I could not do it by myself. Thankfully, my sister Celina agreed to go up with me.

In no time, we were in the bay, and everyone was putting on harnesses and life vests. All of a sudden, I felt faint and began to turn white. In fact, I do not know how I remained on my feet. In the meantime, our boat was speeding along at 50 mph, and we were told to move to the back of the boat and sit down with our legs extended and arms around a bar.

As the parachute was unhooked, we lifted upward into the air. I was yelling and holding my sister's hand and arm. Once we reached our peak, the air was calm, and for miles I could see our side of the island. I could even see Haleakala Volcano on the other side of the island. The ride was awesome, and after a few seconds I was less nervous and even smiled for a photographer in a not-too-distant helicopter who was taking pictures that we could eventually buy.

The sailing through the air lasted only a short ten minutes. As the boat pretended to drop us where we had begun, we were surprised when the boat accelerated, and once again we were lifted into the wide blue. Being more alert and not so scared this time, I could look down into the water beneath me. My sister and I did see, we thought, two small tiger sharks swimming below us in the water. I certainly was glad I was in the air, not in the water.

Finally, we were dropped onto the beach, and after many thanks and compliments to our boatmen, we left to explore other cool things to do in this paradise away from home. Riding along, I was feeling proud and confident because I had faced two of my fears, and I was ready to tackle the world.

Name ___________________________________

Read each question. Circle the letter beside each correct answer.

1. The story is mainly about:
   A. a young girl who learns to parasail in Hawaii
   B. all the fun activities to do on vacation in Hawaii
   C. two sisters bonding on a vacation in Hawaii
   D. building self-confidence and refusing fear

2. Referring to the sentence, "When we arrived at the beach, our coordinator told us that the boat was malfunctioning, so we would have to wait until another boat was ready,"—what are the context clues for the word "malfunctioning"?
   A. wait, another boat
   B. we would have
   C. arrived at the beach
   D. coordinator told us

3. An antonym for the word "alleviate" is:
   A. lessen
   B. relieve
   C. worsen
   D. stop

4. With whom does the speaker in the story share her vacation?
   A. sister
   B. family
   C. sister and brother
   D. no one

5. A conclusion one might draw after reading the story is that:
   A. The narrator will never want to parasail again.
   B. Hawaii is the right place to vacation if one wants a variety of activities.
   C. The narrator will be more successful in life because she is learning self-confidence.
   D. The narrator will become more difficult for her parents to handle.

6. Which one of the following events happened last?
   A. I tried to calm my nerves by swimming and playing on the beach.
   B. We left to explore other cool things to do in this paradise.
   C. I was yelling and holding my sister's hand and arm.
   D. My sister and I did see two small tiger sharks swimming below us in the water.

Total Problems: **Total Correct:** **Score:**

Read the passage and answer the questions on the following page.

Slippery Stairs

Wood can be very pretty in a home. It can be used for almost everything: tables, floors, desks, chairs, or in my case, stairs. To keep wood clean, one has to clean and polish it often. This is where my story begins.

One night, as my mom and dad were leaving to go to the mall, they left instructions for me to clean and polish the stairs. The words "clean" and "polish" are still debated—even today.

I am the type of person who doesn't mind hard work, so I grabbed a broom and first swept the stairs. I have always enjoyed being told that I have done a good job, so that night I wanted to do a good job. Therefore, I was determined to make the old wooden stairs look new again. I must have spent two hours rubbing and polishing the steps over and over again, as I listened to Spanish CDs. I am in my third year of Spanish at Rockwell Middle School, and that night I thought I could accomplish two things at once. You know—two birds with one stone.

When my parents arrived home around 9:00 that night, they promptly noticed the stairs and were terribly impressed with how they were shining. After thanking me and beginning to ascend the steps, my parents said good-night as I retreated to the den where I had been watching a movie. I had just sat down when I heard a yelp and a series of thuds coming from the direction of the stairs. Running into the living room, I saw my dad lying at the bottom of the stairs.

My dad had slipped on the stairs and had made a thunderous acrobatic tumble to the bottom. Of course, my first impulse was to burst into laughter since he appeared to be unhurt, but I didn't. The mental image of my dad rolling down the stairs made self-control almost impossible as I attempted to help him to his feet.

Once he was on his feet and had regained feeling in his whole body, he began to laugh, and I joined him. However, it was our laughing that brought my mom onto the scene, since she had not heard the series of thuds. When she realized what had happened, she was furious with me and scolded me for polishing the stairs. She said someone could have been seriously hurt, and I should have known better. I told her I did what I thought I was told to do. She insisted she never told me to polish the stairs and that I had misunderstood.

During the next week, there were a few other minor falls. My dad especially was very careful on the stairs. One night, just to irritate my mom, my dad threw a heavy cardboard box down the stairs to **simulate** his fall. Thinking my dad had once again fallen, my mom ran to the stairs, only to find the box at the bottom and my dad at the top of the stairs, waving and yelling. It was hilarious; at least, my dad and I thought so.

Name ________________________________

Read each question. Circle the letter beside each correct answer.

1. The main idea of the story is:
   A. Stairs need to be cleaned and polished regularly.
   B. Misunderstandings can sometimes be humorous.
   C. Parents can sometimes be wrong.
   D. Chores can be entertaining.

2. Another word for "simulate" is:
   A. different
   B. add
   C. initiate
   D. imitate

3. Which one of the following statements is not true?
   A. I listened to French CDs.
   B. She was furious with me and scolded me for polishing the stairs.
   C. My first impulse was to burst into laughter since he appeared to be unhurt.
   D. The words "polish" and "clean" are still debated, even today.

4. Which one of the following events happened first?
   A. My dad threw a cardboard box down the stairs to simulate his fall down the stairs.
   B. I had just sat down when I heard a yelp and a series of thuds.
   C. It was our laughing that brought my mom onto the scene.
   D. They left instructions for me to clean and polish the stairs.

5. Where were the speaker's parents when the speaker cleaned and polished the stairs?
   A. in the den
   B. at the mall
   C. at a PTA meeting
   D. at a business meeting

6. Which one of the following words was the basis for the conflict in the story?
   A. polish
   B. thuds
   C. stairs
   D. broom

7. Which one of the following words does not describe the speaker?
   A. hard worker
   B. determined
   C. lazy
   D. industrious

Total Problems:	Total Correct:	Score:

Read the passage and answer the questions on the folowing page.

The Mud Puppy

Last summer, two of my friends and I got the urge to fish at Guntersville Lake. Since this was the first summer that we were old enough to drive, we thought this would be something new and fun to do. Furthermore, the lake is quite large, sprawling around the whole city, and walking around with a tackle box and a rod would take too much time and would be too cumbersome. Therefore, we decided that it would be in our best interest to bring a fishing boat with us.

Since I had always enjoyed fishing and was hoping to learn how to duck hunt, the idea of being able to fish anywhere on the lake was just about the best thing I could imagine. I had been fishing out of an old, leaky aluminum boat in our cow pond. The boat was still in fair condition, I thought, so my friends and I attempted to make it "seaworthy." The blissful thought of fishing on the lake in a decent boat must have clouded our judgment. After a coat of paint, a new transom, and an attempt to stop the leaking rivets, we realized that she was beyond repair.

Disappointed but not beaten, we diligently searched to find a suitable boat. Occupying all our free moments, the search became an obsession. If the search were not punishment enough, we were often teased by finding a boat that seemed to meet our meager requirements, only to find it lacking in some major area or two. The trailer would be missing, or it would be two hundred dollars too expensive. On one occasion, we called with intention to purchase, only to learn that the boat had already been sold. However, just when we thought that we should give up on the boat, things changed.

Chad, one of my friends, spotted a boat in a nearby neighbor's yard. The boat was a fourteen-foot long, flat-bottomed, deep-hulled boat, complete with a trailer. It wasn't in mint condition, but I could see potential right away. Getting her back to operating condition would be a big job, but it could and would be done if the owner would sell her.

Initially, my two friends and I had agreed to a three-way partnership in the boat if we found one. However, my friends' funds were almost **depleted**, and if the boat were to be bought, I would be the one to do it.

Soon after Chad had told me about the boat, I stopped by the house to inquire. The old man who owned the boat said he hadn't used it in twenty years and would be happy just to get it out of his yard. I asked him how much he would take for the boat, and he replied that I could just take it. It was free!

Once home, I quickly began work on my "new" boat. She needed a transom, a good wire brushing, two new trailer tires, a paint job, and lights. But most importantly, she needed a motor, which I finally found after searching the classifieds. After a few weeks of hard work and a little money, she was ready for the water. However, she did need one more important thing: a name. Since the boat was small and slow, an intimidating name wouldn't be right. I would be using it for fishing and duck hunting, so she would be operating in some mud and muck. Therefore, the only name I thought fitting was "The Mud Puppy."

Name ______________________________

Read each question. Circle the letter beside each correct answer.

1. "The Mud Puppy" is the name of a:
   A. little dirty puppy
   B. car
   C. brown guppy
   D. boat

2. The main idea of the story is:
   A. Fishing and hunting at Guntersville Lake is fun.
   B. Believing something and then working to obtain it is rewarding.
   C. Finding something to occupy one's time in the summer is important.
   D. Buying a fishing boat is a difficult process.

3. "The old man who owned the boat said he hadn't used it in twenty years and would be happy just to get it out of his yard. I asked him how much he would take for the boat, and he replied that I could just take it. It was free!" After reading the story, one might infer that the old man gave the speaker the boat because:
   A. The boat was stolen and the old man wanted to get rid of it.
   B. The old man was moving away.
   C. The man was getting old, and the boat required many repairs.
   D. The old man's wife insisted he give the boat away.

4. Another word for "depleted" is:
   A. stolen
   B. depended
   C. exhausted
   D. doubled

5. Which one of the following is not what the boat needed?
   A. lights
   B. transom
   C. paint job
   D. kitchen

Total Problems:	Total Correct:	Score:

Name ______________________________

Read the passage and answer the questions on the following page.

A Boring Vacation

Sam sighed loudly as he entered the den. He hoped to get his mother's attention by doing this. He was bored, and she always had good ideas for things to do. She didn't wake up, though. He told Andy, his older brother, that he was going bike riding, and he sprinted away.

It was summer, and there wasn't much for a thirteen-year-old to do in rural Mississippi. He was biking down the road, thinking of what to do next, when suddenly he hit a hole and swerved off the road.

"Whoa!" Sam yelled as his bike headed toward a freshly dug ditch. He had managed to pull himself out when he heard something.

"Hey, kid, go away!" yelled a voice from the other side of the road. It appeared to be coming from Blue Creek.

"Who...who's there?" Sam called cautiously.

"None of your business!" yelled the same voice. "Now, beat it before you get yourself hurt!"

Sam swiftly ran to his bike, but before he could leave, a car stopped and yelled at the unseen voice. "You'll be sorry for this!" yelled someone from inside the car.

The car then sped away quickly. Without hesitating, Sam pedaled as fast as his long legs would go. When he arrived home, he threw his bike on the front porch and rushed inside.

"Sam Timon, look at yourself! You're a mess! Now, go clean up and get ready for supper," his mom commanded as he entered the house.

Sam did as his mother said, but he was eager to tell everyone about his adventure. At dinner he explained what had happened. He told about the voice, but no one seemed to care. He cared though, and he was determined to find out who the **enigmatic** voice was at Blue Creek.

The next day, thinking his bike would make too much noise, he hiked to Blue Creek. Shortly after he arrived, he saw two men talking, and he recognized one of the voices as the man he had heard yesterday. Furthermore, he saw shovels lying on the ground beside the two men. He had seen a movie in which two men buried stolen money they had acquired after robbing the local bank. Sam's heart jumped.

Sam listened to the men's conversation. Before he could stop himself, he sneezed, and both men jumped. The man whose voice he had discerned quickly walked in his direction; however, Sam was too scared to move.

"Sorry about the scare I gave you yesterday, kid. We've been digging a ditch here, and we were just about ready to let the water rush in. I just wanted to keep you from getting hurt," the familiar voice said in a pleasant tone.

Feeling a surge of relief overcome his body, Sam was grateful the man had explained everything—almost everything. "What about the car that drove by yesterday and yelled at you?" he asked curiously.

"Oh! That was one of my neighbors. He has tried to stop this ditch all along, but we really do need it. Without it, the creek would overflow and wash the road away," the man explained convincingly. Sam talked a few more minutes with the men and then left for home.

"Now," he thought to himself as he walked along, "it will be a boring vacation." A few minutes later, reflecting on what had happened the past two days, again Sam thought to himself, "Well, maybe, a boring vacation isn't so bad."

Name ____________________________________

Read each question. Circle the letter beside each correct answer.

1. Sam found out that the two men were actually:
   A. hiding money which they had stolen from a bank in town
   B. hiding from the police because they had committed a crime
   C. digging a ditch to prevent the road from washing away
   D. planting trees to help the environmentalists in the local community

2. "Feeling a surge of relief overcome his body, Sam was grateful the man had explained everything—almost everything." What are the context clues that suggest the meaning of the word "grateful"?
   A. overcome, body
   B. explained, his
   C. almost, everything
   D. feeling, surge, relief

3. Which statement is true?
   A. Sam heard a voice that said, "Hey, boy, go away!"
   B. Sam didn't ride his bike to Blue Creek the second day.
   C. The story takes place in rural Missouri.
   D. The first day at Blue Crane, Sam yelled, "Who...who's there?"

Total Problems: **Total Correct:** **Score:**

Read the passage and answer the questions on the following page.

An Unusual Day

The sun leaked through the tiny cracks in my blinds. The morning sun was shining brightly when I opened my eyes. The room was a pale yellow with tiny chips missing at the edge of the baseboard across from my bed. This was the first night in my new apartment, and I loved it. The apartment building was only three blocks from the bookstore where I worked part-time. The small store housed hundreds of books, new and old. I was in charge of keeping all of them in order. It was a nice job for a full-time student.

One morning as I was casually strolling down the street to work, I happened to bump into an older gentleman. As I was making apologies and attempting to hide my embarrassment, I looked at the man's face. It was worn and haggard, but at the same time the face seemed familiar. I asked his name, and he was obliged to give it to me. He was Don Phillips. I had heard that name before, but I couldn't recall where or when.

I walked to the bookstore with Don's face vividly fixed in my mind. I couldn't shake his worn and tired features from my memory. For the remainder of the day, I worked and tried to forget about the old man. Later that evening after arriving home, my grandmother called to ask about my new apartment. We chatted for half an hour because my grandmother is my best friend. As we were saying good-bye, I asked to speak to Grandfather.

At first, our conversation was the usual talk about how he was doing and how things were on the farm. I knew that my grandfather had lost a close friend a few weeks ago and was still morose; however, he said he was feeling better. I had never met his best friend or known his name. However, as we talked, the name of his friend came out and, astonishingly, his name was Don Phillips. For a brief minute, I paused and reflected again on what had occurred that morning.

I told Grandfather about the man who said his name was Don Phillips. He found it quite odd that there would be another man in our small town with the same name. Nevertheless, he told me to put the incident behind me because a man with the same name was possible. I promised I would, and we said good-bye.

That night I tossed and turned because I knew the man I had met that morning was someone from my past. I wanted answers, but I didn't know how I would get them. I would have to wait for Grandfather to **relinquish** his grief over his lost friend. In the meantime, I thought it would be inappropriate to ask further questions about Grandfather's friend. However, the way Grandfather described his friend matched the description of the Don Phillips I had met that day. How strange, I thought.

Name ________________________________

Read each question. Circle the letter beside each correct answer.

1. A conclusion one might draw concerning Don Phillips is:
   A. Grandfather's friend actually did not die and is still living in the town.
   B. Grandfather's friend did die, and the stranger the speaker meets is just someone with the same name.
   C. The speaker misunderstood the old stranger she met on the street.
   D. The old man the speaker meets is suffering from a mental illness, and whenever he meets someone he always gives a different name.

2. Another word that means the same as the word "morose" is:
   A. sick
   B. crazy
   C. sad
   D. happy

3. "I looked at the man's face. It was worn and haggard, but at the same time the face seemed familiar." A context clue that might suggest the meaning of the word "haggard" is:
   A. worn
   B. dirty
   C. handsome
   D. clean

4. Where did the speaker meet the stranger with the name Don Phillips?
   A. at the bookstore one morning
   B. at Grandfather's house
   C. on the street on the way to work
   D. at the university one day

5. Which one of the following statements is not true?
   A. The speaker lives three blocks from the bookstore.
   B. The speaker's grandfather lives on a farm.
   C. The speaker has a grandmother and a grandfather.
   D. The speaker is a part-time student and works at a job part-time.

6. A word or expression that means the opposite of the word "relinquish" is:
   A. surrender
   B. keep
   C. give up
   D. offer

7. The first thing the speaker noticed after bumping into the stranger was:
   A. the stranger's neck
   B. the stranger's face
   C. the stranger's clothes
   D. the stranger's broken arm

Total Problems: **Total Correct:** **Score:**

Read the passage and answer the questions on the following page.

Shocking Mistake

It was an early summer morning in August, and Mark Williams hurriedly threw his things into his bag. He was getting ready to leave his small North Carolina town for college, and he was overly excited about his newfound freedom. Mark and his best friend Cory planned on attending New York University together. There, they hoped to become experts in a medical field and eventually have a practice of their own. The two college freshmen also wanted to have the time of their lives.

"Mark, are you ready?" his mom yelled from the bottom of the stairs. "Cory's waiting."

About that time, Mark came jolting down the stairs. "Bye, Mom. I love you," Mark said as he gave his mom a big bear hug. "Let's go, Cory," he finally said with an eager look on his face. Then the two jumped into Cory's convertible and were on their way.

Many hours later, after some intense driving, they arrived at New York University. The enormous buildings that blanketed the campus astonished and overwhelmed the new college students, and they could not wait to get to the place where they would be living for the next four years. After a quick registration, they decided it would be wise to find their dormitory room because it was getting late.

Mark removed a tiny slip of paper from his wallet, which read *1407 Maple Lane.*

"That should be easy enough," Mark said to Cory. "We're already on Maple Lane. All we have to do is find the building." They drove down the street approximately ten blocks before coming upon a small sign in a yard which read *1407 Maple Lane.*

"Wow!" Cory exclaimed.

"This must be an awesome dorm!" Mark agreed. They pulled into the entrance, and the colossal gates opened wide, allowing them to enter. Cory drove slowly around the circular driveway and came to a stop at the front door. As they stepped out of the car and walked hesitantly through the large, wooden doorway at the front of the building, both of the boys were overcome with an **eerie** feeling. Darkness fell around this building and there was only a minute amount of light at various points in the corridor. Sensing that it was too late to officially check in, they explored a long hallway and decided that this was a wing of bedrooms. Finding a suitable spacious bedroom, Mark and Cory decided to get some rest, since they had been terribly busy all day.

Both fell into a deep sleep until about midnight when they were awakened by footsteps. They decided to investigate and possibly meet some other students who were probably coming in from a late night date. Rushing downstairs, they were **bewildered** to see an older man and woman in their pajamas in the kitchen. Even more so, the older couple were startled to see the boys.

After some immediate verbal reactions and responses, amidst a threat from the older man, the boys quickly discovered they were not in the college dormitory. They had made a big mistake and were supposed to be at 1107 Maple Lane, not 1407.

Name ______________________________

Read each question. Circle the letter beside each correct answer.

1. The main idea of this story might be:
   A. Registering for college for the first time is exciting.
   B. Drive carefully when you are away from home.
   C. It is important to pay close attention to details and directions.
   D. Leaving home for college after high school can be fun.

2. A synonym for the word "bewildered" is:
   A. puzzled
   B. angry
   C. scared
   D. happy

3. Why were Mark and Cory leaving North Carolina?
   A. to go on a vacation
   B. to go on a business trip
   C. to visit their grandparents
   D. to go to college

4. Referring to the sentences: "As they stepped out of the car and walked hesitantly through the large, wooden doorway at the front of the building, both of the boys were overcome with an eerie feeling. Darkness fell around this building and there was only a minute amount of light at various points in the corridor,"—the context clues for the meaning of the word "eerie" are:
   A. around this building
   B. darkness fell … only a minute amount of light
   C. as they stepped out
   D. walked slowly

5. What address were Cory and Mark supposed to find?
   A. 1407 Maple Lane
   B. 1107 Mableton Lane
   C. 1107 Maple Lane
   D. 1407 Marble Lane

Total Problems: **Total Correct:** **Score:**

Read the passages. Circle the letter beside each correct answer.

Dyslexia

People with dyslexia often have difficulty distinguishing the smallest sound unit of language, the phoneme. Because of this handicap, they are frequently unable to connect letters with sounds, distinguish between sounds or separate the different parts of a word. And, they and often mix word parts together. Word omission when reading or writing is another common symptom associated with those having dyslexia. Nonetheless, this is often overlooked as simply being grammatical errors that could easily be corrected. The same goes for those people who confuse letters in many words while in the process of reading or writing. Reversals may be the most well-known symptom of this disorder, although it is commonly not present in its victims. Reversals occur when a person writes or reads backwards. This also carries over into math, where numbers could be transposed in a problem, causing it to be incorrect. Generally speaking, poor spelling and poor handwriting tend to accompany these previously described symptoms.

1. Which of the following statements is false?

A. People with dyslexia are unable to connect letters with their sounds.
B. Reversals occur when a person writes or reads backwards.
C. Reversals may be the least well-known symptom of dyslexia.
D. People with dyslexia are unable to separate the different parts of a word.

Archaeology

Archaeology is the study of objects left by earlier people, including artwork, buildings, clothing, pottery, and tools. Archaeologists trace the development of cultures by studying the things those people made and used. Such objects help them determine what early social life may have been like. Archaeologists are able to study an artifact at a site and piece together an entire way of life for those people who left it behind. Archaeologists study techniques for finding, excavating, dating, and analyzing material remains of past societies, as well as major trends in cultural evolution. They try to pinpoint a particular time and place as gleaned from the artifacts and fit them into a bigger picture of what life would have been like.

2. Which of the following statements is true?

A. Archaeologists study the development of languages over a period of time.
B. Archaeologists paint pictures of how they perceive life to be.
C. Archaeology is the study of animals and plants.
D. Archaeologists study major trends in cultural evolution.

Total Problems: **Total Correct:** **Score:**

Name ______________________________

Read the passages. Circle the letter beside each correct answer.

Jazz Music

At the beginning of the twentieth century, fully developed jazz music emerged. New Orleans, Louisiana was the musical home of the first notable players of jazz, including Louis Armstrong and Jelly Roll Morton. In 1917, the Original Dixieland Jazz Band was the first jazz band to record their music. Mamie Smith recorded in 1920, and these recordings of ragtime, blues, and jazz popularized the music to the public. The 1920s have been referred to as the Jazz Age. Commercial radio stations played live performances. New Orleans, Memphis, St. Louis, Chicago, and New York City were all thriving jazz centers. A lot of musicians from New Orleans migrated to Chicago and then to New York City. As jazz advanced from relatively simple music played by people who often could not read music to a more sophisticated form, large groups of jazz musicians began to play together. This was modeled after society dance bands, forming the popular big bands of the 1930s, leading to the "swing" era.

1. Which one of the following statements is true?
 A. New York was the musical home of Louis Armstrong.
 B. The 1930s has been referred to as the Jazz Age.
 C. Memphis and New Orleans were thriving jazz centers.
 D. In 1927, the Original Dixieland Jazz Band was the first jazz band to record.

Capital Punishment

Capital punishment refers to the execution of a person found guilty of a very serious (or capital) crime. There are several forms of execution that are used. Though lethal injection is becoming the method of choice, the electric chair and the gas chamber are both still used. For most of American history, the death penalty has been a state and local issue. Criminals are tried and convicted depending on local laws and customs. In 1968, few Americans supported the death penalty. Many people believed the death penalty would be permanently abolished. Between the 1980s and 1990s, more people in the United States began to support capital punishment.

2. The word "capital" in "capital punishment" refers to the word(s):
 A. guilty
 B. serious
 C. lethal injection
 D. electric chair

Total Problems: **Total Correct:** **Score:**

Read the passage and answer the questions on the following page.

Oprah Winfrey

Oprah Winfrey was born into poverty in the state of Mississippi on January 29, 1954. Her parents meant to name her Orpah after a woman in the Bible, but they misspelled it. In Oprah's early teens she moved to live with her mother in Milwaukee. At the age of fourteen, she was forced to move in with her father in Tennessee or be sent to a "home."

Her father instituted strict discipline, which turned Oprah's life around for the better. At the age of nineteen, she went to work at a local radio station as a reporter and enrolled in Tennessee State University to study speech and performing arts. In 1978 she went to work for a chat show in Baltimore—"People Are Talking." The management stated that they did not really know what to think of her. However, the viewers loved her and the show's ratings reflected it.

In 1984 she accepted a job as a host of *A.M. Chicago*, which was scheduled opposite of Phil Donahue's top-rated national talk show. Within months Oprah's show was in close competition with Donahue's. Her open and casual style contrasted with that of Donahue's strict formal method.

Oprah received a part in Steven Spielberg's movie *The Color Purple* for which she won an Oscar for best supporting actress. The publicity from the movie launched her show to a national level now called *The Oprah Winfrey Show*. During her first year, the show grossed over $120 million, but she herself only received $30 million. She began a company called Harpo Productions (Oprah spelled backwards) and eventually bought her program from ABC. In 1996, Oprah's show brought in an estimated $97 million.

Read each question. Circle the letter beside each correct answer.

1. All of the following are true except:
   A. Oprah lived with her mother in Milwaukee.
   B. Oprah's name at birth was supposed to have been Orpah.
   C. In 1987, Oprah went to work for a chat shop in Baltimore.
   D. Oprah won an Oscar for her role in *The Color Purple*.

2. "Oprah received a part in Steven Spielberg's movie *The Color Purple* for which she won an Oscar for best supporting actress. The publicity from the movie launched her show to a national level now called *The Oprah Winfrey Show*." What are the context clues that suggest the meaning of the word "publicity"?
   A. supporting, in, movie
   B. received, best, from
   C. launched, national level
   D. part, won, Oscar

3. Oprah is connected in some way to all of the following states except:
   A. Illinois
   B. Florida
   C. Maryland
   D. Tennessee

4. Which of the following is true for Oprah when she was fourteen years old?
   A. She was forced to move in with her father.
   B. She began a company called Harpo Productions.
   C. She went to live with her grandfather in Tennessee.
   D. She went to work at a local radio station as a reporter and attended school.

5. The impetus that launched Oprah's Show into the national spotlight was:
   A. *People Are Talking*
   B. *The Color Purple*
   C. Tennessee State University
   D. *Phil Donahue Show*

6. The word "home" in "She was then forced to move in with her father in Tennessee or be sent to a 'home'" is probably a reference to:
   A. her mother's home
   B. her grandfather's home
   C. a mental institution
   D. a foster home

Total Problems: **Total Correct:** **Score:**

Read the passage. Circle the letter beside each correct answer.

Eldrick "Tiger" Woods

Eldrick "Tiger" Woods was born on December 30, 1975. He is the son of Earl and Kultida Woods. He was nicknamed "Tiger" after a friend of his father's from Vietnam, Vuong Phong, whom his father had also given that nickname. He was raised in the town of Anaheim, California. Earl Woods believed that his son was special from birth. He noticed that Tiger would sit in the garage and watch Earl hit golf balls into a net. So, by the time he was old enough to get out of the high chair, Tiger had a golf swing.

There was no one who doubted Tiger's skill when Tiger showed them that he could play golf. By age 3, Tiger could shoot 48 for nine holes and appeared in *Golf Digest* at age 5. He won the Optimist International Junior tournaments six times at ages 8, 9, 12, 13, 14, and 15. He also won the Insurance Youth Golf Classic at age 14, when he was the youngest ever to win that title. He won his first U.S. Junior Amateur the next year, 1991, and had seven additional victories. Two years later he had achieved seven more titles, including two U.S. Junior Amateurs. In 1994 he was selected as man of the year by *Golf World*.

Tiger attended Stanford University, and in his second year he had eight victories in 14 tournaments and finished lower than third only twice. He was then chosen for the Fred Haskins and Jack Nicklaus College Player of the Year awards. Then, in his junior year of college, he dropped out to become a professional golfer.

1. At 14, Tiger was the youngest golfer ever to win the:
   A. U.S. Junior Amateur Contest
   B. Optimist International Junior Tournament
   C. Insurance Youth Golf Classic
   D. *Golf Digest* award

2. All of the following are true except:
   A. Tiger Woods won the Optimist International Junior Tournament six times.
   B. In 1993, Tiger was selected man of the year by *Golf World*.
   C. By age 3, Tiger could shoot 48 for nine holes.
   D. Tiger dropped out of college his junior year to become a professional golfer.

Total Problems: Total Correct: Score:

Name ____________________________________

Read the passages. Circle the letter beside each correct answer.

The Golden Retriever

The golden retriever is an intelligent, well-built dog with a golden, wavy coat. It is a truly superior hunting dog with a highly developed sense of smell and great intelligence, which makes it easy to train. The dog is also known for its endurance, excellence in swimming, and ability to retrieve. Its calm, gentle, loyal, and sensitive nature makes the dog an ideal family companion. It is a popular contender in obedience circles and has gained recognition as a guide dog for the blind in recent years. The golden retriever is a symmetrical, powerful, active dog—not clumsy. It is very alert and self-confident.

1. Which one of the following statements is not true?

A. The golden retriever is a symmetrical, yet clumsy dog.
B. The golden retriever is a great hunting dog with a great sense of smell.
C. The golden retriever is an excellent swimmer.
D. The golden retriever is used as a guide dog for the blind.

Vitamin A

Vitamin A, one of the first vitamins discovered, is required for a healthy immune system, vision, growth, and reproduction. Perhaps the best known role of vitamin A is its effect on vision. Vitamin A forms a pigment in the eye called visual purple that is required for night vision. Vitamin A is very effective in increasing resistance to diseases and infections. Population studies in developing nations have demonstrated that vitamin A reduces death by increasing resistance to infections. In addition, vitamin A increases the production of antibodies and various disease-fighting cells. With those factors, vitamin A supports a healthy immune system and is also very effective in fighting against cancerous cells. It blocks cancerous cells in cultures and even blocks malignancy in animals exposed to cancer-causing agents. Therefore, vitamin A can be referred to as the wound-healing vitamin.

2. Vitamin A does all of the following except:

A. support a healthy immune system and work effectively in fighting cancerous cells
B. increase the production of antibodies and various disease-fighting cells
C. build healthy red blood cells
D. form a pigment in the eye called visual purple

Total Problems:	**Total Correct:**	**Score:**

Read the passage. Circle the letter beside each correct answer.

Nashville: "Athens of the South"

Located on the Cumberland River in the north central part of the state, Nashville, the capital of Tennessee and home of the Grand Ole Opry, is a frequent stop for tourists. Nashville was actually founded in 1779 as Fort Nashborough in honor of the Revolutionary War General Francis Nash. It was renamed Nashville in 1784.

Because of its many educational institutions and numerous buildings constructed in the Greek Revival style, Nashville has been called the "Athens of the South." A replica of the Athenian Parthenon, built in 1897, commemorates Tennessee's statehood.

Among the city's institutions of higher learning are Vanderbilt University and Fisk University. East of the city is The Hermitage, home-place of the nation's seventh president, Andrew Jackson. During Jackson's lifetime, The Hermitage was known as a place of Southern hospitality. Today, the tradition continues as The Hermitage opens its doors to over 250,000 visitors annually.

An important manufacturing center, Nashville produces chemicals, food products, shoes, machinery, automobile glass, metal products, apparel, textiles, and airplane parts. The city has the nation's second largest recording industry and produces the largest volume of country music records. Nashville is also a major publishing center, particularly for religious literature.

1. Nashville has:
- A. one of the major publishing centers, particularly for religious literature
- B. numerous buildings constructed in the Roman Revival style of architecture
- C. the home of the nation's seventeenth president
- D. the nation's largest recording industry

2. An important manufacturing center, Nashville produces all of the following except:
- A. metal products
- B. airplane parts
- C. automobile glass
- D. tractor tires

3. The popular entertainment home for country music in Nashville is:
- A. The Hermitage
- B. Athenian Parthenon
- C. The Grand Ole Opry
- D. Fort Nashborough

Total Problems: **Total Correct:** **Score:**

Name ________________________________

Read the passage. Circle the letter beside each correct answer.

Hong Kong, China

Hong Kong is situated about ninety miles southeast of Canton, China. Hong Kong was a colony of Great Britain until July 1, 1997, when the Chinese government took control of the city. It has one of the highest population densities in the world (5,412 persons per square mile). About 98% of the population of 6.7 million are Chinese. Most of the people in Hong Kong work in factories, the shipping industry, or for the government. About 60,000 Hong Kong residents emigrate each year, mostly to North America and Australia, seeking better economic opportunities.

Hong Kong was originally acquired by Great Britain because of its magnificent natural harbor (Victoria Harbor). During the nineteenth century, it was the main **entrepôt** for Western commerce with China. One-third of China's imports and exports still pass through the port. Hong Kong's success in exporting manufactured goods to Europe and North America attracted substantial investment by American and Japanese firms. Leading exports are now textiles and clothing, electronics, clocks and watches, domestic appliances, and plastics.

Hong Kong lies just below the Tropic of Cancer. The summer months are hot and humid with a mean temperature of 86°F. Typhoons sometimes occur during this season. The winter months are cooler with a mean temperature of 60°F.

1. Under whose protection and government was Hong Kong until 1997?
   A. China
   B. Australia
   C. Great Britain
   D. United States

2. Which one of the following statements is true?
   A. About 90% of the population of 6.7 million are Chinese.
   B. Hong Kong was originally acquired by Great Britain because of its natural harbor.
   C. The summer months are hot with a mean temperature of 80°F.
   D. Hong Kong has one of the lowest population densities in the world.

3. Another word for "entrepôt" is:
   A. intermediary center of trade and shipping
   B. enterprise
   C. entrepreneur
   D. porter

Total Problems: **Total Correct:** **Score:**

Refer to the recipe to answer the questions. Circle the letter beside each correct answer.

Preparing Banana Pudding

1/2 cup sugar
2 tablespoons all-purpose flour
1/4 teaspoon salt
2 cups milk
3 large eggs, separated
1 teaspoon vanilla extract
1 (12-ounce) package vanilla wafers
4 large bananas
1/4 cup sugar
1/2 teaspoon vanilla extract

Combine the first 3 ingredients in the top of a double boiler; gradually add milk, stirring well. Bring water to a boil; reduce heat to low, and cook, stirring constantly, until mixture is thickened. Beat egg yolks at medium speed until thick and pale. Gradually stir about one-fourth of hot mixture into yolks; add to remaining hot mixture; stir constantly. Cook over low heat, stirring constantly, for 5 minutes or until mixture is thickened. Remove from heat; stir in 1 teaspoon vanilla. Cool for a few minutes. Layer one-fourth of vanilla wafers in an ungreased, 3-quart baking dish. Slice 1 banana, and layer over wafers. Pour one-fourth of custard mixture over the banana slices. Repeat layers 3 times, using remaining vanilla wafers, banana slices, and custard mixture. Beat egg whites at high speed until foamy. Gradually add 1/4 cup sugar, 1 teaspoon at a time, beating until stiff peaks form and sugar dissolves (2 to 4 minutes). Add 1/2 teaspoon vanilla, beating well. Spread meringue over custard, sealing to edge of the dish. Bake, uncovered, at 350° for 20 minutes or until lightly browned. Servings: 6 to 8

1. What is the first thing you do?
A. Beat the yolks at medium speed.
B. Bring water to a boil.
C. Combine the first 3 ingredients.
D. Gradually add milk, stirring well.

2. After adding 1/4 cup sugar, what do you do next?
A. Spread meringue over the custard.
B. Beat until stiff peaks form.
C. Bake for 20 minutes.
D. Slice one banana and add slowly.

3. How many minutes do you bake the banana pudding?
A. 20 minutes
B. 2 to 4 minutes
C. 3 minutes
D. 5 minutes

4. What does "extract" mean in "vanilla extract"?
A. the outermost or farthest point
B. to infer or estimate
C. very unusual; exceptional
D. concentrated substance from food

Total Problems: **Total Correct:** **Score:**

Refer to the recipe to answer the questions. Circle the letter beside each correct answer.

Chocolate Lovers' Brownies

Brownie Ingredients
2 cups sugar
1 cup butter, softened
4 eggs
4 1-ounce squares unsweetened chocolate, melted and slightly cooled
$2\frac{1}{2}$ cups sifted flour
$\frac{1}{4}$ teaspoon salt
$\frac{1}{4}$ teaspoon baking powder
2 teaspoons vanilla extract
1 cup broken walnuts or pecans

Glaze Ingredients
6 tablespoons butter
1 cup semisweet chocolate chips
2 teaspoons vanilla extract

Preheat the oven to 350°. In a large bowl, cream together the sugar and butter until fluffy. Beat in eggs until well blended; add melted chocolate. Sift the flour, measure, then sift again with the dry ingredients and add to the creamed mixture along with vanilla and nuts. Spread in a greased and floured 9" x 12" baking pan and bake for 25 to 30 minutes or until no imprint is left when touched with finger. Do not overbake.

If a glaze topping is desired, combine the butter and chocolate chips in the top of a double boiler; add vanilla and blend thoroughly. Pour gently over the brownies and spread by tipping the pan. Cut when cool, as interiors are still moist when fresh from the oven. Yield: 24 brownies

1. What is the first step in the recipe?
A. Preheat the oven to 350°.
B. Sift the flour, measure, then sift again.
C. Beat in the eggs until well blended.
D. Cream together the butter and sugar.

2. All of the following ingredients are needed except:
A. 2 cups sugar
B. 1 cup butter
C. 1 cup marshmallows
D. 1 cup broken walnuts or pecans

3. After the eggs are blended, you should:
A. Sift the flour.
B. Spread in a greased baking pan.
C. Preheat the oven to 350°.
D. Add the melted chocolate.

4. This brownie recipe will make:
A. 12 brownies
B. 25 brownies
C. 24 brownies
D. 30 brownies

Total Problems: **Total Correct:** **Score:**

Refer to the recipe to answer the questions. Circle the letter beside each correct answer.

Macaroni and Cheese Casserole

$1\frac{1}{2}$ cups macaroni, uncooked
2 tablespoons butter or margarine
2 tablespoons all-purpose flour
1 cup milk
1 cup shredded, processed American cheese
$\frac{1}{4}$ teaspoon salt
$\frac{1}{4}$ teaspoon pepper
$1\frac{1}{2}$ cups **diced** cooked ham
2 tablespoons prepared horseradish
2 teaspoons prepared mustard

Cook the macaroni according to the package directions; drain and set aside. Melt butter in a heavy saucepan over low heat; add flour, stirring until smooth. Cook 1 minute, stirring constantly. Gradually add milk; cook over medium heat, stirring constantly, until mixture is thickened and bubbly. Add cheese, salt, and pepper, stirring until cheese melts. Stir in ham, horseradish, and mustard. Combine macaroni and sauce, stirring well. Pour into a greased 1-quart baking dish. Bake, uncovered, at 350° for 20 minutes or until thoroughly heated. Servings: 4

1. What does the word "diced" mean?
A. thrown
B. cooked
C. cut
D. eaten

2. After draining and setting aside the cooked macaroni, the next step is:
A. Cook the macaroni for one minute longer.
B. Add flour to a saucepan.
C. Add milk and cook over medium heat, stirring constantly.
D. Melt the butter in a saucepan and add flour.

3. How long and at what temperature do you bake the casserole?
A. 4 minutes at 350°
B. 20 minutes at 350°
C. 20 minutes at 300°
D. 10 minutes at 350°

4. The only ingredient not used in the preparation of the macaroni and cheese casserole is:
A. all-purpose flour
B. shredded, processed American cheese
C. green bell peppers
D. butter or margarine

Total Problems: **Total Correct:** **Score:**

Read the passage. Circle the letter beside each correct answer.

San Francisco: The Contemporary City

San Francisco, located on the coast of California, occupies a peninsula that is the southern landfall of the Golden Gate channel. This narrow channel connects the Pacific Ocean with San Francisco Bay, one of the world's most beautiful, natural harbors. Spanning the channel is the Golden Gate Bridge, long a symbol of the city as the U.S. port of entry on the Pacific coast.

A popular tourist city, San Francisco offers spectacular views from its forty-three hills. The weather remains mild throughout the year, with average monthly temperatures differing little from January (49°F) to September (64°F).

San Francisco today has an economy very dependent on white-collar industries. A skyline of high-rise office buildings, dominated by the Transamerica Building and the Bank of America tower, marks the downtown **terminus** of Bay Area Rapid Transit (BART), one of the country's most modern high-speed mass-transit systems. On Russian and Nob Hills, stately mansions have been replaced by luxury apartment buildings and hotels. The last three cable car lines, now designated as national historic landmarks, still cross the hills. To the east of Nob Hill lies Chinatown, one of the largest Chinese communities outside of Asia. Fisherman's Wharf, a commercial fishing port established by nineteenth-century Italian immigrants, is now a row of restaurants, souvenir shops, and motels. The Cannery and Ghirardelli Square, once fruit canning and chocolate plants, respectively, now house specialty shops, restaurants, and art galleries. Within San Francisco Bay is the former federal prison, Alcatraz.

1. Which one of the following is not a famous landmark in San Francisco?
- A. Golden Gate Bridge
- B. Alcatraz
- C. State Capitol
- D. Fisherman's Wharf

2. Another word that means the same as "terminus" is:
- A. destroyer
- B. end
- C. continuous
- D. plan

3. San Francisco has:
- A. one of the world's most beautiful man-made harbors
- B. two cable car lines as designated national historic landmarks
- C. a former federal prison located outside the San Francisco Bay
- D. one of the largest Chinese communities outside of Asia

Total Problems: **Total Correct:** **Score:**

Name ______________________________

Refer to the advertisement to answer the questions. Circle the letter beside each correct answer.

Announcing the opening of our new location!

Central Park West

Always the best selections for teenagers!

Ross Glider-Blades
All Sizes & Styles
Wheel & Bearing Packages
$179.95

Sealeg Tennis Shoes
All Sizes Available
White, Sport White, or Black
$129.95

Rodeo Jeans
Baggy-fit in Stone, Straight-leg, and Loose-fit
100% Cotton; Imported
$49.95

Apple Blossom Knit Shirts
100% Combed Cotton
Banded Short Sleeves & Straight Bottom with Side Vents
$29.95

2900 West Paces Ferry Road, NW
Special Store Hours: 9:00 AM – 7:00 PM Monday – Saturday

1. Where would you most likely find this advertisement?
   A. telephone book
   B. early childhood magazine
   C. local newspaper
   D. almanac

2. This advertisement mainly appeals to:
   A. middle-aged parents
   B. teenagers
   C. grandparents
   D. young, single adults

3. All of the following items are advertised except:
   A. Sealeg Tennis Shoes
   B. Ross Glider-Blades
   C. Apple Blossom Knit Shirts
   D. Rogers Wash & Wear Jeans

Total Problems: **Total Correct:** **Score:**

Name ________________________________

Read the poem. Circle the letter beside each correct answer.

A Southern Spring

Robins and dogwoods out on the lawn,
Green grass and little calves out in the pasture.
Tulips and daffodils springing up everywhere.
Flowering cherry trees and pears adorn the landscape.
Sunrise mornings and sunset evenings
reflect the Earth's bounteous fortunes.
Nature, untamed and wild,
like an eagle soaring freely overhead.
I want to run and play today
beside the creek or river.
I want to catch the wind and drink the rain.
I want to feel the sun and smell the land.
I want to be today.

1. Referring to the line: "Nature, untamed and wild, like an eagle soaring freely overhead,"—because nature is compared to an eagle, the writing technique is called a:
   A. metaphor
   B. simile
   C. personification
   D. pun

2. Another word that means the same as "bounteous" is:
   A. wild
   B. beautiful
   C. abundant
   D. sad

3. The main idea of the poem is:
   A. All the animals and plants in nature are out in the springtime.
   B. Nature is untamed and wild.
   C. The author enjoys living in the South and gardening.
   D. The speaker wants to participate in the new life and beginning of spring.

Total Problems:	Total Correct:	Score:

Name ______________________________ **Reading a Mileage Chart**

Refer to the mileage chart to answer the questions. Circle the letter beside each correct answer.

If you are planning a trip by car, you may want to consult a mileage chart like the one below. To read the mileage chart: 1) Locate one of the cities in the left-hand column. 2) Then, go across that row to the column headed by the other city's name. The number shown is the distance in road miles between the two cities.

Road Mileage	Baltimore MD	Charlotte NC	Detroit MI	Louisville KY	Norfolk VA	Phoenix AZ	St. Louis MO
Baltimore, MD	N/A	435	534	617	232	2,348	845
Boise, ID	2,397	2,359	1,968	1,887	2,546	998	1,629
Cheyenne, WY	1,662	1,624	1,233	1,152	1,811	916	894
Dallas, TX	1,367	1,032	1,211	836	1,353	1,067	631
Fargo, ND	1,362	1,432	933	946	1,549	1,691	861
Memphis, TN	913	628	757	382	899	1,478	285
Washington, DC	36	398	534	615	195	2,350	845
Yosemite, CA	2,900	2,658	2,446	2,313	2,929	685	2,055

1. How many miles is it from Fargo, ND, to Norfolk, VA?
A. 1,691 B. 1,353 C. 1,549 D. 899

2. How much farther is it from Yosemite, CA, to Charlotte, NC, than from Yosemite, CA, to St. Louis, MO?
A. 503 B. 603 C. 602 D. 703

3. How much greater is the distance from Washington, DC, to Detroit, MI, than from Memphis, TN, to St. Louis, MO?
A. 349 B. 241 C. 248 D. 249

4. How many miles would you travel from Dallas, TX, to Louisville, KY?
A. 836 B. 946 C. 1,211 D. 353

5. The Kretzmers are traveling from Baltimore, MD, to Phoenix, AZ. The Spencers are going from Baltimore, MD, to Cheyenne, WY. How much farther will the Kretzmers travel than the Spencers?
A. 686 miles B. 868 miles C. 790 miles D. 680 miles

Total Problems: **Total Correct:** **Score:**

Name ______________________________

Refer to the graph to answer the questions. Circle the letter beside each correct answer.

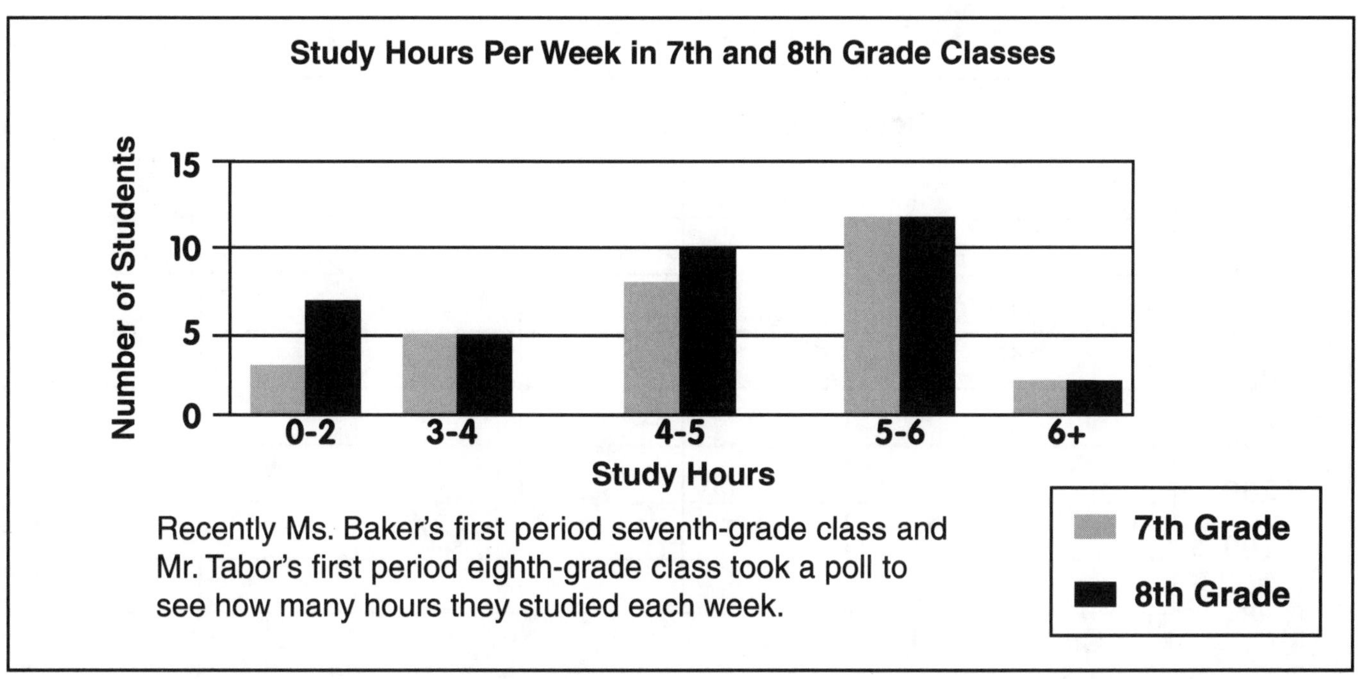

Recently Ms. Baker's first period seventh-grade class and Mr. Tabor's first period eighth-grade class took a poll to see how many hours they studied each week.

1. How many students in both the seventh and eighth grades study between 3-5 hours per week?
   A. 8 B. 10 C. 12 D. 15

2. How many more eighth-grade students study between 4-5 hours per week than seventh-graders?
   A. 2 B. 4 C. 6 D. 8

3. How many eighth-grade students study 3 hours or more a week?
   A. 10 B. 15 C. 22 D. 29

4. How many seventh-graders study between 5-6 hours per week?
   A. 8 B. 10 C. 12 D. 15

5. What was the most common amount of time for eighth graders to study?
   A. 0-1 B. 3-5 C. 4-5 D. 5-6

Total Problems:	Total Correct:	Score:

Name ______________________________

Refer to the graph to answer the questions. Circle the letter beside each correct answer.

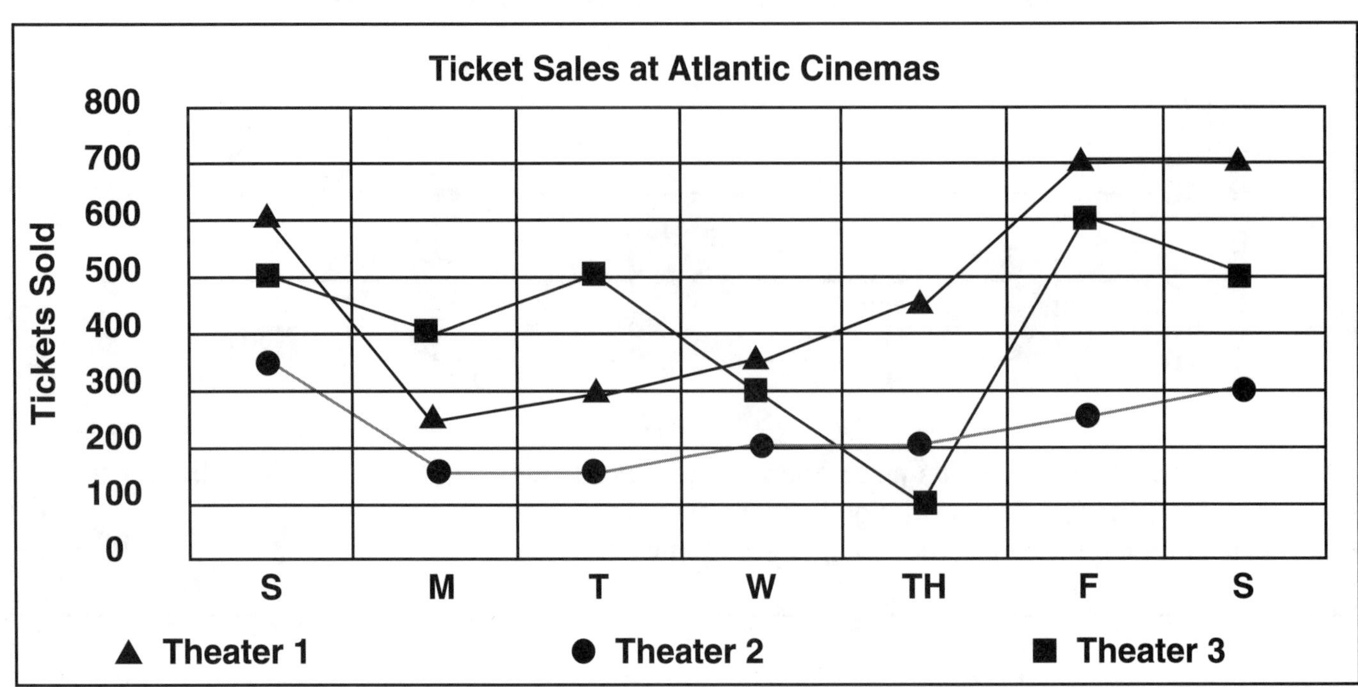

1. What was the total number of tickets sold for Theater 3 for the entire week?
   A. 2,600 tickets
   B. 2,700 tickets
   C. 2,800 tickets
   D. 2,900 tickets

2. For the week of sales, how many more movie tickets did Theater 1 sell than Theater 3?
   A. 450 tickets
   B. 350 tickets
   C. 1,300 tickets
   D. 1,750 tickets

3. If the price per movie ticket is $7.00, what would be the total amount of sales for Theater 3 on Friday, Saturday, and Sunday?
   A. $5,250
   B. $8,400
   C. $11,200
   D. $14,000

4. Which theater sold the most tickets for the week, and how many tickets did it sell?
   A. Theater 3—2,900
   B. Theater 2—1,600
   C. Theater 1—3,350
   D. not given

Total Problems: Total Correct: Score:

Name ______________________________

Refer to the graph to answer the questions. Circle the letter beside each correct answer.

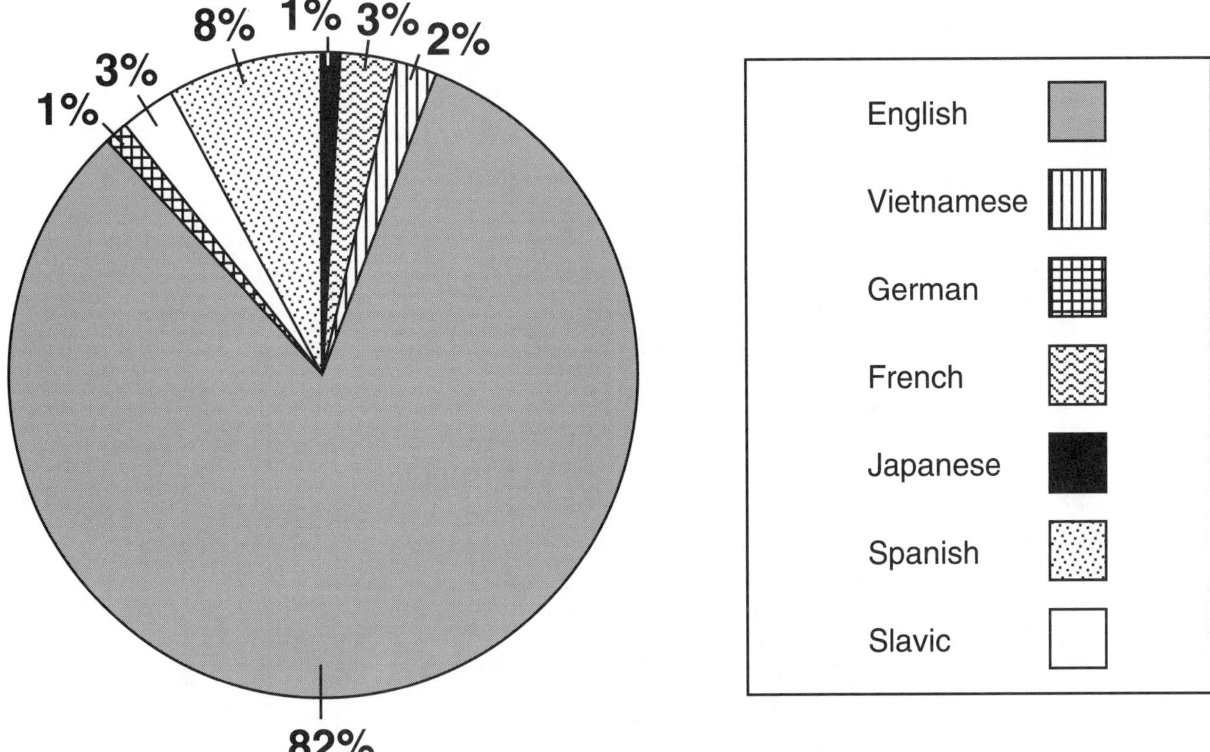

Languages Spoken at Carmel Middle School

1. If there are 1,500 students attending Carmel Middle School, how many students represent English as their primary language?

A. 1,150 B. 1,230 C. 1,520 D. 1,860

2. How many students represent Slavic, Spanish, and French as their primary speaking languages?

A. 180 students B. 200 students
C. 210 students D. 220 students

3. If there were 15 more students who speak Spanish and Slavic as their primary languages and you were to subtract that number from the number of students who speak English and Vietnamese, how many students would you have?

A. 1,080 B. 1,045 C. 1,085 D. 1,055

4. If you were to add the number of students whose primary languages are Spanish, Japanese, and German, how many more students speak these combined languages than those of Slavic, Vietnamese, and French?

A. 50 B. 20 C. 80 D. 30

Total Problems:	Total Correct:	Score:

Name ______________________________

Refer to the map to answer the questions. Write your answers in the blanks provided.

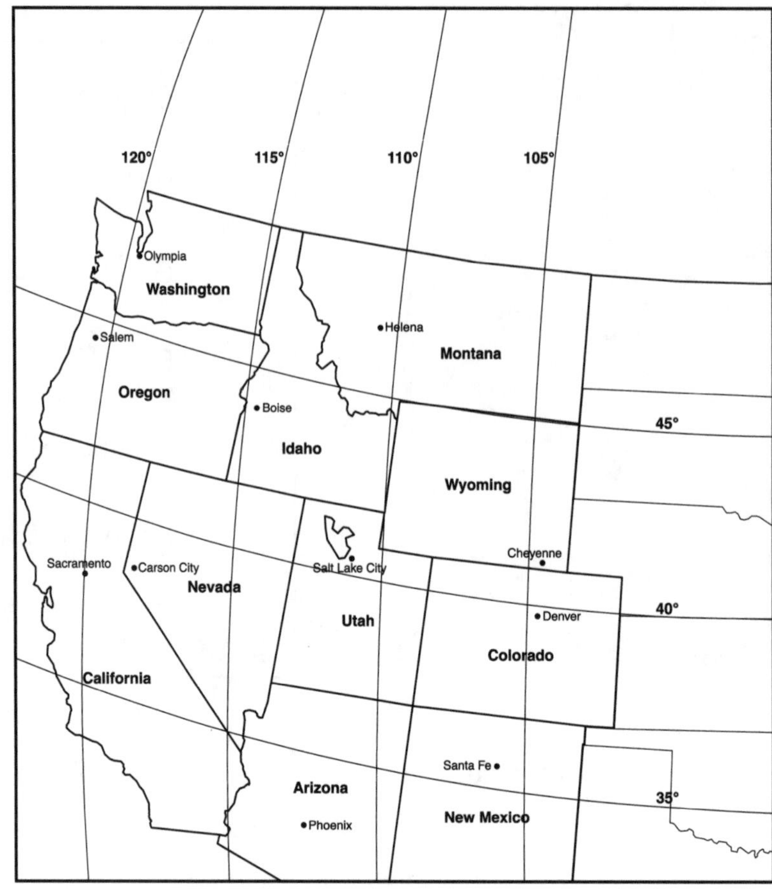

1. Salem, Oregon is almost directly on the _______ parallel.
2. The state of Wyoming is located between 41°N parallel and _______ parallel.
3. Boise, Idaho is south of the _______ parallel.
4. Denver, Colorado is almost directly on the _______ parallel of latitude.
5. What city in California is located between the 35°N and 40°N parallels? _______________
6. The boundary between Wyoming and Montana is formed by the _______ parallel.
7. Helena, Montana is in which direction from the 45°N parallel? _______________

Total Problems:	Total Correct:	Score:

Name ______________________________ **Reading a Map: Midwestern United States**

Refer to the map to answer the questions. Circle the letter beside each correct answer.

1. Ohio's western boundary is formed by the state of:
   A. Indiana B. Michigan C. Illinois D. Wisconsin

2. What river forms the boundary between Missouri and Illinois?
   A. Wabash River B. Mississippi River C. Missouri River D. Platte River

3. The capital of Missouri is:
   A. Kansas City B. Topeka C. Jefferson City D. Des Moines

4. The northern boundary of Texas is partly formed by what river?
   A. Red River B. Missouri River C. Platte River D. Oklahoma City

5. The northeastern border of Michigan is formed by which lake?
   A. Lake Erie B. Lake Superior C. Lake Michigan D. Lake Huron

Total Problems: **Total Correct:** **Score:**

Read each question. Circle the letter beside each correct answer.

Library and Reference Materials

1. If your science teacher suggested that your class plant a corn field in the spring at the right time of the moon, you would consult:
   A. *National Geographic Atlas* B. *World Almanac and Book Of Facts*
   C. *Bartlett's Book of Quotations* D. *Reader's Guide to Periodical Literature*

2. In which section of the newspaper would you find movie listings?
   A. sports section B. classified section
   C. front page D. entertainment section

3. If you had to find a word that has the same meaning as "dismay," you would look in:
   A. an encyclopedia B. an atlas
   C. a thesaurus D. the telephone directory

4. Where in a book do you find the title, author, and publisher (on one page)?
   A. index B. glossary
   C. title page D. table of contents

5. If your history teacher asked you to bring in recent information about the secretary of state's most recent political trip abroad, you would probably look in:
   A. an encyclopedia B. a card catalog
   C. a dictionary D. a newspaper

6. Your family is going to the island of Crete. You don't know where this island is located. To find out where this island is located, you would probably look in:
   A. a card catalog B. a thesaurus
   C. an atlas D. a biographical dictionary

7. You are doing research on the Washington Monument in Washington, DC. To find general information on this famous monument, you could look in:
   A. a thesaurus B. an international who's who
   C. an encyclopedia D. Reader's Guide to Periodical Literature

8. Your English teacher asked you to find the meaning of "homonym." You would look in:
   A. an atlas B. a thesaurus
   C. a dictionary D. an encyclopedia

Total Problems:	Total Correct:	Score:

Name ___________________________________

Read the dictionary entry below. Refer to the entry to answer the questions. Circle the letter beside each correct answer.

Reading the Dictionary

issue (ish´oo) ***n.*** to go out. 1. an outgoing; outflow. 2. a place or means of going out; outlet; exit. 3. a result; a consequence. 4. offspring; a child or children. 5. profits, as from property; proceeds. 6. a point or matter under dispute. 7. a sending or giving out. 8. the entire amount put forth and circulated at one time: as, the May issue of a magazine, an issue of bonds. 9. in medicine, a discharge of blood, pus, etc. ***v.i.*** {-sued, suing},1. to go, pass, or flow out; emerge. 2. to be descended; be born. 3. to result, as from a cause. 4. to end (in); result, as in an effect. 5. to come as revenue. 6. to be published; to be put forth and circulated. ***v.t.*** 1. to let out; discharge. 2. to give or deal out: as, to issue supplies. 3. to publish; put forth publicly or officially, as periodicals, bonds, an edict, etc. -at issue, in dispute; to be decided. -join issue, to meet in conflict, argument, etc. -take issue, to disagree. -is su a ble, ***adj.*** -is´su er, ***n.***

1. Which numbered definition means "a matter under dispute"?
   A. 2
   B. 8
   C. 6
   D. 5

2. What is the part of speech for the word "issue" which means "a consequence"?
   A. adjective
   B. noun
   C. adverb
   D. verb

3. In the following sentence, "The president issued a proclamation announcing that all people would be allowed to vote,"—what part of speech is the word "issued"?
   A. verb
   B. noun
   C. adverb
   D. adjective

4. What is definition # 2 for the word "issue" used as a transitive verb?
   A. to let out
   B. to discharge
   C. to give or deal out
   D. to put forth officially

Total Problems: **Total Correct:** **Score:**

Refer to the Reader's Guide to Literature entry and the sample title page information to answer the questions. Circle the letter beside each correct answer.

Reader's Guide to Literature

Nursing Your Sick Dog [taking care of your dog] R. Schwartz. il *All About Pets* v. 34 no. 14 p. 54-59 O 10 99

1. What is the name of the article in the entry above?

A. "All About Pets"
B. "R. Schwartz"
C. "Nursing Your Sick Dog"
D. "Taking Care of Your Dog"

2. Where is the article found, according to the entry above?

A. Nursing your sick dog
B. Taking care of your dog
C. R. Schwartz
D. *All About Pets*

3. In which month and year is the article found?

A. November, 1999
B. October, 1999
C. November, 1954
D. November, 1959

Title Page

All About Soccer

Terry Payne
Anna Harris

International Publications, Inc.

4. International Publications, Inc., is the name of the:

A. book
B. city
C. author
D. publisher

5. Who wrote the book?

A. Terry Payne
B. Terry Harris and Anna Payne
C. Anna Harris and Terry Payne
D. Anna Harris

Total Problems: **Total Correct:** **Score:**

Name ________________________________

Refer to the card catalog entry to answer the questions. Circle the letter beside each correct answer.

Computerized Card Catalog

Title information: Mr. Penn Visits London / by Pat Henry, with introduction by Jorge Fincher

Author: Henry, Pat 1953

Published: London: Red Press, © 1979

Physical description: 214 pp.: 22 cm

Notes: Mark Penn, a newcomer to the big city, becomes the talk of all the young women, until one night an incident happens at a gala event and the identity of young Mark becomes questionable.

Notes: Interest grade level: 7-8

Subject: Humorous fiction

1. According to the card catalog, what do we know about the book?
- A. The book is about a newcomer called Mark Penn.
- B. Mark Penn dresses as a clown and juggles at a gala event.
- C. At a gala event, a group of rich women discover the true identity of Mark.
- D. One late night a very serious situation occurred at a party.

2. The person who wrote *Mr. Penn Visits London* is:
- A. Pat Fincher
- B. Red Press
- C. Pat Henry
- D. Jorge Fincher

3. How many pages does the book contain?
- A. 1,979
- B. 214
- C. 23
- D. 222

4. For what grade level is this book intended?
- A. 6-7
- B. 5-8
- C. 7-8
- D. 6-8

5. What is the name of the publishing company?
- A. London Press
- B. Jorge Fincher
- C. Red Press
- D. London Red Press

Total Problems: **Total Correct:** **Score:**

Name ______________________________

Refer to the table of contents from the book *Ancient Egypt and Greece* to answer the questions. Circle the letter beside each correct answer.

Table of Contents

1. If your teacher asked you to find information on the building of the Great Pyramid of Giza, you could probably find information on what pages?

A. 19-25
B. 6-11
C. 26-32
D. 48-53

2. If you were seeking information on the origin of the Olympic Games, in which chapter would you most likely find the information?

A. History of the Olympic Games
B. Greek Statues at Olympia
C. The Great Pyramid of Giza
D. Mesopotamia

3. From which chapter would this sentence most likely come? "To protect the mummy from damage, it was placed in a coffin-like container called a sarcophagus. The style, shape, and decoration of the sarcophagus changed over the years."

A. Ancient Egyptian Burials
B. Inside the Great Pyramid
C. The Great Pyramid of Giza
D. Mummies

Total Problems: **Total Correct:** **Score:**

Refer to the memo to answer the questions. Circle the letter beside each correct answer.

Reading a Memo

DATE: May 12
TO: Virginia Powell, General Manager
FROM: Stacie Kendall, Inventory Clerk
RE: Inventory Receiving Report

After checking the receiving report and the inventory in the warehouse, I have found the following **discrepancies** on our recent order:

1 case of notebook paper #017358
2 cases of computer paper #480571
6 packages of blue ballpoint pens #264325
3 cases of third-cut file folders #832109

Please find attached my count, as well as the inventory records.

Attachment

1. What is the item number (#) for the computer paper?
A. 832109
B. 264325
C. 017358
D. 480571

2. Another word that means the same as “discrepancy” is:
A. inconsistency
B. amount
C. agreement
D. addition

3. Who sent the memo?
A. Virginia Powell
B. Attachment
C. Stacie Kendall
D. not given

4. The purpose of the memo was to relate information concerning:
A. stolen goods
B. inventory
C. new warehouse
D. closeout sale

Total Problems: **Total Correct:** **Score:**

Reading an Index

Refer to the index to answer the questions. Circle the letter beside each correct answer.

1. If you wanted to find information on the atom bomb that was used by a former U.S. president, on what pages would you look?

A. 753-754 B. 624-625
C. 225-226 D. 658-659

2. If you were researching Hawaii and you wanted to find information on travel in the state, on what pages would you look?

A. 166-167 B. 69-70
C. 693-694 D. 691-692

3. On what page would you look to find the main office for the TVA?

A. 721 B. 276
C. 431 D. not given

4. Which one of the following statements about the index is not true?

A. Information on Harriet Tubman can be found on page 387.
B. Information on Tuskegee Institute in Alabama is found on page 721.
C. Trolley cars and turnpikes are found on pages 274 and 465.
D. The Twentieth and the Twenty-fourth Amendments are found on pages 214 and 730.

Total Problems: **Total Correct:** **Score:**

Name ______________________ **Following Directions**

Refer to the U.S. map to answer each question. Write your answers in the spaces provided.

1. In which direction would you travel if you went from Kentucky to Utah? west
2. Which two states are directly east of California? Nevada, Arizona
3. Which state is north of North Carolina? Virginia
4. Name the states that border Minnesota on the west. North Dakota, South Dakota
5. Which state is between Mississippi and Georgia? Alabama
6. Which two states are directly south of New York? Pennsylvania, New Jersey
7. In which direction would you travel to go from New Mexico to Wisconsin? northeast
8. Which three states border Louisiana? Arkansas, Texas, Mississippi

Total Problems: Total Correct: Score:

Name ______________________ **Finding the Main Idea**

Read each passage. Circle the letter beside each correct answer.

The Flute

The flute, one of the oldest instruments ever created, has been around for the last several hundred years. The word *flute* is derived from the Latin word *flatus* which means "blowing" or "breathing." Playing the flute takes more air to make a sound than any other instrument. A person may often feel faint because of the amount of air needed to produce a good tone. However, this is a normal occurrence for any flautist seeking a balanced tone.

The tone of a flute is the most admired because it does not have a "squeak" or "honk" as does a clarinet or trumpet. At times, the flute may produce a high-pitched tone which is often described as sounding like a bird and is the most difficult tone to produce successfully. Other times the flute may produce a low-pitched tone, which is the most beautiful tone the flute makes. This type of musicality is most often used in music written in a minor key. Flute music can be the most enjoyable and the most challenging to play.

1. The main idea of the passage is that:
   A. The flute has been around for hundreds of years.
   B. The word "flute" comes from the word "flatus" which means "blowing."
   (C) Flute music can be most enjoyable and the most challenging to play.
   D. At times, the flute sounds like a bird.

Nuclear Energy

According to the Nuclear Energy Institute, nuclear energy has perhaps the lowest impact on the environment of any energy source. Nuclear energy does not emit harmful gases; it isolates its waste from the environment and requires less area to produce the same amount of electricity as other sources. The long periods of operation and the large size of the plants have enabled United States nuclear energy plants to provide a dependable and economical source of electricity for the United States and the world. Unlike some other energy sources, nuclear energy is not subject to unreliable weather or climate conditions, or dependence on foreign suppliers.

2. The main idea of this paragraph is that:
   A. Nuclear power is an amazing accomplishment.
   B. Nuclear power needs a large supply of water to cool nuclear components.
   C. Nuclear power plants are built near lakes, rivers, or oceans.
   (D) Nuclear energy is a safe, economical, and dependable source of electricity.

Total Problems: Total Correct: Score:

Name ______________________ **Finding the Main Idea**

Read each passage. Circle the letter beside each correct answer.

Baseball

Baseball is one of the oldest and most popular spectator sports. During the early 1800s, baseball developed into the game it is today. Although its exact origins are obscure, it is thought by many to have been invented in 1839 by Abner Doubleday. He was a Union officer in the American Civil War. However, it more likely evolved from a popular eighteenth century English game called "rounders." Baseball became popular during the American Civil War, among both Northern and Southern troops.

The Cincinnati Red Stockings was the first professional baseball team and began play in 1869. Later, a separate league for black athletes produced many fine players in the early twentieth century. Jackie Robinson began playing for the Brooklyn Dodgers in 1947. This opened the doors for the racial integration of major-league baseball. He was one of the greatest players in the Negro Baseball Leagues and the first African-American player to play in the modern major leagues.

1. The main idea of this passage is:
   A. Baseball may have been by invented civil war troops.
   B. Baseball more likely evolved from "rounders," a Brooklyn game.
   (C) The passage relates the possible origins and history of major-league baseball.
   D. Jackie Robinson opened the door for racial integration in baseball.

Disorders of Eating

Using food to meet emotional needs is a learned behavior that can become addictive and lead to disordered eating habits. There are several different types of eating disorders. These include *anorexia nervosa*—an extreme food restriction, and *bulimia nervosa*—a cycle of binge eating followed by vomiting, laxatives, or excessive exercise to get rid of food. Other types include *food addiction*—eating when not hungry, and *disordered eating*—an unbalanced attitude about food, weight, and the body that leads to very rigid eating and exercise habits. People can gain freedom from these learned behaviors by retraining themselves to use food to meet only physical needs and by learning healthy ways to satisfy their emotional needs.

2. The main idea of this passage is:
   A. Disordered eating is a balanced attitude about food and the body.
   (B) Disordered eating is a learned behavior which can be unlearned.
   C. Proper dieting and exercise is important.
   D. Binge eating is unhealthy.

Total Problems: Total Correct: Score:

Name ______________________ **Identifying Inferences**

Read each passage. Circle the letter beside each correct answer.

An *inference* is an assumption based on the facts and evidence that are given.

Organ Transplants

There are over 60,000 people awaiting organ donations in the United States alone. The need for organ donations is urgent! There is a new name added to the organ transplant waiting list every sixteen minutes. This means ninety people a day and 32,850 people a year are being added to the waiting list. Living in this fast-paced world is a contributing factor to the increasing number of people awaiting transplants. This fast-paced lifestyle leads to the consumption of a poor diet which contributes to declining health. Stress can also be a major factor in the inability to fight disease. Together, these factors lead to the need for more organ transplants.

1. After reading the passage, one can infer that:
   A. A poor diet can contribute to declining health.
   B. Stress is a factor in the reduced ability to fight disease.
   (C) If stress and a fast-paced lifestyle are absent, the chances of needing an organ transplant are reduced.
   D. Over 60,000 people are awaiting organ donations.

The Human Brain

The human brain controls bodily functions efficiently. Most health professionals believe that a positive attitude can boost a person's immune system. People can choose to practice either a positive or negative outlook. Optimism will yield a healthier person, just as a negative outlook can result in an unhealthy person. The brain has a major influence on bodily function; therefore, feelings, emotions, and states of mind have a major effect on the body's well-being.

2. An inference in the passage above is that:
   A. The body controls the thinking process.
   B. Immunity is acquired only after one has all the shots required.
   C. The body controls feelings, emotions, and states of mind.
   (D) If a person has a positive attitude, the mind and body work together more efficiently.

Total Problems: Total Correct: Score:

Name ______________________ **Identifying Inferences**

Read each passage. Circle the letter beside each correct answer.

An *inference* is an assumption based on the facts and evidence that are given.

Peer Pressure

It is a common misconception that all peer pressure is negative. Some peer pressure is actually beneficial to adolescents. Peers are necessary in helping adolescents make a successful transition from dependency on their parents to self-reliance. Peers can and do act as positive role models. Peers can and do demonstrate appropriate social behaviors. Peers often listen to, accept, and understand the frustrations and challenges associated with being a teenager.

Peer pressure plays a beneficial part in every adolescent's development and involvement with others. Parents play a big part in helping the adolescent with the transition from dependency to independence. Parents can make sure that their child does not fall under the influence of a detrimental peer group. They can create strong bonds with their child, build the child's self-esteem, take an interest in what their child does, and set good examples.

1. An inference found in the second paragraph above is that:
   (A) If kids have strong, supportive parents, peer pressure will most likely be positive.
   B. Parents cannot help that much in the transition from teenager to adult.
   C. Peer pressure is necessary, but not so positive.
   D. Peers often listen to concerns associated with being a teenager.

Obsessive-Compulsive Disorder

Obsessive-compulsive disorder, also known as OCD, is a biologically based anxiety disorder. This disorder can begin in childhood and persist throughout a person's life. The individual who suffers from OCD sometimes has thoughts of a disturbing nature, which may cause the person to repeat certain activities in an attempt to relieve anxiety. Symptomatic of the disorder are unwelcome thoughts and a compulsion to carry out meaningless rituals, such as guarding against danger or excessive cleaning. The paradox is that those with the disorder realize the rituals are irrational, yet find themselves repeating them in an effort to relieve anxiety. These symptoms can interfere with thinking, reasoning, and/or life functioning. Medical science has developed drug therapies and behavior modification techniques that have helped people with this disorder.

2. An inference you can make is that:
   A. Obsessive-compulsive disorder is a mild childhood disorder.
   B. Obsessive-compulsive disorder may begin only in one's adult life.
   C. We often find ourselves in ordinary situations.
   (D.) Someone who is obsessed with cleaning or guarding against danger may have OCD.

Total Problems: Total Correct: Score:

Name ______________________ **Arranging the Sequence**

As you read the letter, keep in mind the clues that let you know the order in which the events happen. Then, circle the letter beside each correct answer.

Dear Jay,

I have been at Camp Mountain Lake for three weeks, but already it seems much longer. There have been so many activities and fun things to do that time has passed very quickly. I apologize for not having written sooner, but I haven't had much spare time.

The seventh- and eighth-grade boys are living in the Pioneer cabins this summer—quite different from last summer. Do you remember last summer? As a Pioneer, we are allowed a later curfew, and we are allowed to water-ski. You should be here. Terry Schwartz, a Cub from North Miami, fell last week on an overnight camping trip and broke his arm. The Cubs had gone camping in Pisgah, where we went last summer, and they were swimming and playing at Sliding Rock when he slipped and fell. That place is so much fun. I wore out the bottoms of two pairs of jeans there last summer, and this summer the Pioneers have been there once. I could spend a week there sliding down those rocks into the frigid icy water. The water must be around 32 degrees. Wouldn't you agree?

Tonight is the big bonfire on the hill where we did our outdoor drama last summer. Every cabin must participate in tonight's event. Do you remember the play last year? It was hilarious.

Write me when you get a chance. I will be home in about five weeks, and we will do some cool things before school begins. I must go and prepare for tonight.

Your friend,
Spencer

1. Which one of the following events happened first?
   (A) . . . and they were swimming and playing at Sliding Rock when he slipped and fell.
   B. . . . fell last week on an overnight camping trip and broke his arm.
   C. Tonight is the big bonfire.
   D. Every cabin must participate in tonight's event.

2. Which one of the following events happened last?
   A. Terry Schwartz fell last week on an overnight camping trip and broke his arm.
   B. I wore out two pairs of jeans.
   (C.) . . . we will do some cool things before school begins.
   D. . . . where we went last summer, and they were swimming and playing . . .

Total Problems: Total Correct: Score:

Name ______________________ **Arranging the Sequence**

As you read the passage, keep in mind the clues that let you know the order in which the events happen. Then, circle the letter beside each correct answer.

Just in Time

After a week of working hard and making friends in the town of Carmen Bajo, we took a day to explore the shops of Otavalo. After three hours of riding, we were all ready to take a walk, but not quite like the one I was about to take when I jumped off the bus into the busy streets of Quito, Ecuador.

It was just before dark when I looked up to see a cute, young boy who said his brother wanted to see me. I saw in his hand my address, in my own writing, and I realized who my little visitor must be. He was the brother of my friend, Fernando, who had come to visit me on my last night there.

Fernando walked around the block to find a taxi for his brother; we then decided to take a different route back. After walking for a while, we realized that this was not the road we were looking for. We were definitely lost! We ran for a while because I did not want to be late, especially since I was not supposed to have left the hotel in the first place, much less with a boy. Finally, we saw a police officer standing on a street corner, and he directed us to the hotel. When we could see the hotel down the road, we said our good-byes until next year, and I walked back to the hotel just in time. Everything had worked out perfectly; that is, until I looked down to see I was still holding his jacket, and he had already gotten into a taxi and disappeared.

1. Which one of the following events happened first?
   A. Everything had worked out perfectly; that is, until I looked down to see . . .
   (B.) After three hours of riding, we were all ready to take a walk . . .
   C. We ran for a while because I did not want to be late, especially since I was . . .
   D. We saw a police officer standing on a street corner, and he directed us to the hotel.

2. Which one of the following events happened last?
   A. . . . we saw a police officer standing on a street corner, and he directed us to the hotel.
   B. . . . we were all ready to take a walk, but not quite like the one I was about to take . . .
   C. We ran for a while because I did not want to be late, especially since I was . . .
   (D.) When we could see the hotel down the road, we said good-bye . . .

Total Problems: Total Correct: Score:

Name ______________________ **Drawing Conclusions**

Read the passage. Circle the letter beside each correct answer.

A Bottle of Perfume

Jason Perkins had been a problem student since he set foot into Mrs. Harris's sixth-grade class. Every day he came into class poorly dressed, unclean, and inattentive. Whenever Mrs. Harris marked his paper "unsatisfactory," she thought to herself, "Why is this student wasting my time?"

Soon the Christmas season was approaching, and Mrs. Harris was giving her usual reviews. When she came upon Jason's review, she noticed that other teachers had reviewed him as being "very bright and a joy to have around." Confused, Mrs. Harris looked further into the matter and discovered that Jason had been reared by just his mother until this past summer. However, during the summer, she had passed away and custody had been given to his father who was not interested in raising a child. Mrs. Harris felt badly for not understanding and being more sympathetic.

The day before Christmas vacation, Mrs. Harris opened the presents that the children had brought her. All the presents were neatly wrapped except for Jason's, which was sloppily wrapped in newspaper. As she opened Jason's present, she discovered it was an almost empty bottle of perfume. Being courteous, Mrs. Harris smiled and thanked Jason and sprayed a little perfume on herself. As the children were leaving for Christmas vacation, Jason stopped at her desk and said, "You know, Mrs. Harris, today you smell just like my mother." As Jason walked out of the classroom, Mrs. Harris began to cry.

1. What conclusion had Mrs. Harris drawn before discovering the truth about Jason?
   A. Jason was a poor student who didn't care about school.
   (B.) Because Jason was unclean, inattentive, and poorly dressed, he was not capable of being intelligent and a fun student with whom to work.
   C. Jason's other teachers must have made a mistake in reviewing him.
   D. Jason should have been kept in the fifth grade.

2. What conclusion can the reader make after reading the story?
   A. Mrs. Harris will continue to wonder why Jason is wasting her time in class.
   B. Jason will continue to make unsatisfactory marks in Mrs. Harris's class.
   (C.) Mrs. Harris will become more attentive and helpful to Jason.
   D. Jason will quit school and run away from his father.

Total Problems: Total Correct: Score:

Name ______________________________ **Drawing Conclusions**

Read the passage. Circle the letter beside the correct answer.

The Red Path

One lazy Sunday afternoon, two friends, Randy and Lynn, decided to go hiking at the local state park. The weather was mild and beautiful, so they knew it would be a good day to spend outdoors. After quickly packing a picnic lunch, Randy and Lynn were on their way.

When they arrived, they chose one of the numerous paths available. Each path was marked by different colors of spray paint that marked the trees and plants in the path. It looked as if it would be impossible to get lost, or so they thought.

The path they chose was marked with red paint. Following the path for about fifteen minutes, Randy and Lynn became hungry and decided to stop and eat the picnic lunch. This quickly replenished their energy, and they were ready to continue the hike. As they walked, they enjoyed the majestic mountains, falling leaves, and the bubbling creek. It was a beautiful day, and it did not seem that anything could go wrong. However, as they were enjoying the surrounding nature, they had accidentally wandered onto the orange path.

Feeling that orange would meet back with the red path, they continued on the path. Soon, the orange led to yellow, and Randy and Lynn realized they had no idea where they were going. Eventually, they found signs pointing in opposite directions, so they chose one and hoped for the best. After walking for about two hours, they began to think their beautiful scenery had turned into a horrible prison from which there seemed to be no escape. It would soon be dark and difficult to see the paint colors, so they knew they had to walk fast.

Just when sheer panic and hopelessness were about to take hold, Randy noticed that things were starting to look familiar. All this time, they had just been going in a big circle! There had been no cause for distress; they were not lost after all. After coming to this joyous realization, it took them only about five minutes to find their way back to the car. Randy and Lynn decided it would be awhile before they went hiking again.

1. After reading the above passage, what conclusion can you draw?
   - A. Hiking in a state park can be fun if the weather is mild.
   - B. A person should never hike alone.
   - **(C.)** When hiking in the woods, pay constant attention to where you are going to prevent getting lost.
   - D. Always hike on the red path when you hike in a state park.

Total Problems: Total Correct: Score:

Name ______________________________ **Recognizing Supporting Details**

Read the passage and answer the questions on the following page.

Flitter the Butterfly

Flitter the butterfly was courageous, soaring through the Texas skies all day and night. Sweeping through the big **cumulus** clouds, Flitter never stopped to think about what might lie ahead of her. The other insects, especially George the grasshopper, tried to warn her of the **predators** that might leap at her when she was not paying attention, but Flitter wouldn't bother to listen. She wanted to be adventurous, and she thought the other insects were envious of her.

Besides thinking Flitter was courageous, the insects also thought she had lost her little mind. Flitter was still young and didn't know what other species there were out in the world. However, the insects realized that Flitter would find out eventually, and hoped she would survive.

One day when Flitter was out enjoying her morning flight, she came upon a bird's nest high in a maple tree. Immediately, she flew down into the nest that was occupied by four little birds. Thinking Flitter was their mother, they began snapping their little beaks. Flitter thought they were playing with her, so she began to tease them by swooping down and then flying up into the air. In fact, she was having so much fun she didn't realize what was happening behind her back. Berta, the mother bird, was swooping down intending to use Flitter as the babies' meal.

Flitter looked up just in time to move out of the way of Berta's sharp beak. Flitter started flapping her wings as fast as she could to get away, but immediately Berta gave chase to her. Flitter dove into a tree and into a little hole in the tree trunk. Realizing Flitter had gotten away, Berta returned to her babies.

Slowly, Flitter came out of the hole in the tree trunk and then flew as fast as she could back to her home to find all the other insects waiting on her. Sharing her story with everyone, Flitter appeared to have learned an important lesson that day. Although the insects told Flitter they had been trying to warn her about all the predators, they were still thankful and proud that Flitter had survived that day.

Name ______________________________ **Flitter the Butterfly**

Read each question. Circle the letter beside each correct answer.

1. With whom does Flitter have a dangerous encounter one day on her morning flight?
   - A. George
   - B. Texas
   - **(C.)** Berta
   - D. baby birds
2. Which one of the following words best describes Flitter?
   - A. selfish
   - B. clown
   - C. smart
   - **(D.)** courageous
3. When Flitter escaped her predator, where did she hide?
   - A. hole in the ground
   - **(B.)** hole in the tree trunk
   - C. hole in the cumulus clouds
   - D. hole in the building
4. "Flitter the Butterfly" is a story about:
   - **(A.)** a young insect who learns an important lesson about predators
   - B. a nest of baby birds
   - C. a group of insects who live and work together
   - D. a young boy who learns how to survive in the world
5. Another word for "predator" is:
   - A. Berta
   - B. an animal that chirps
   - **(C.)** a preying animal
   - D. insect
6. How many baby birds were found in the nest?
   - A. 3
   - **(B.)** 4
   - C. 10
   - D. 1
7. George, a friend of Flitter, is a:
   - **(A.)** grasshopper
   - B. snail
   - C. bird
   - D. bug
8. If you are "envious" of someone, you are:
   - A. disliked
   - B. loved
   - **(C.)** jealous
   - D. loathed

Total Problems: Total Correct: Score:

Name ______________________________ **Identifying Figurative Language**

Figurative Language uses devices such as similes, metaphors, personification, and alliteration.
Example: *The girl is beautiful.* (Literal Language)
The girl is like a rose. (Figurative Language)

Read the poems and circle the letter beside each correct answer.

Two Worlds

Between me and the sunset,
every twig jumping out of the blazing orange
like a guardian standing at the portal
between two opposite worlds.
This world has grown familiar;
I am accustomed to its gristmill rhythm.
The other is wild and untamed.
It hasn't learned to be subdued,
forced into ill-fitting fetters.
Wonders lie hidden in the glowing orange,
but is there danger too?

1. In the third line, "like a guardian," is what figure of speech?
   - A. metaphor
   - **(B.)** simile
   - C. irony
   - D. pun
2. Read lines 7-9, "The other . . . fetters." What is the poet saying about the other world?
   - A. It has become too familiar and tame.
   - B. It is between the sun and the moon.
   - **(C.)** It hasn't become routine and tamed.
   - D. It is rhythmical with twigs jumping in the sun.

Frosty

The snowman came last night
and filled the sky with shadows
and covered the ground with white.
He did his job with no mistake,
as he carefully made each snowflake.
And every field that he had chosen
will surely be found frozen.
I watched the snow throughout the day
knowing his gift would not stay
since the sun will come out to melt it away.

3. Why won't the snow stay?
   - A. The snowman will take it with him.
   - B. The rain is going to dissolve it.
   - C. The fields don't like it.
   - **(D.)** The sun will melt it.
4. Who is the "he" referring to in line 4?
   - A. night
   - B. snowflake
   - **(C.)** snowman
   - D. sky

Total Problems: Total Correct: Score:

Name ______________________ **Identifying Figurative Language**

Read the poem and circle the letter beside each correct answer.

An Apple Tree

I have an apple tree
in my garden,
but the apples do not fall
until they are rotten.

They hit the steadfast ground
and burst apart,
seeds floating in the apple
sauce like ships out of port.

Small vessels sailing down
into the soil,
hoping to establish their
colonies on the shore.

The towns will be trees
mirroring life
in the form of rotten fruit
bursting in my garden.

1. In the second stanza, "seeds floating in the apple sauce like ships out of port," what is the dominant figure of speech?
   - A. metaphor
   - B. pun
   - (C.) simile
   - D. personification
2. In the third stanza, what are the "Small vessels"?
   - A. ships
   - (B.) seeds
   - C. trees
   - D. fruit
3. "Small vessels," in the third stanza, is a figure of speech known as a:
   - A. simile
   - B. paradox
   - C. personification
   - (D.) metaphor
4. Referring to the third stanza: What are the "vessels" hoping to accomplish?
   - A. The ships, with people on board, are hoping to establish a new colony.
   - B. The ships are carrying people to Australia—the down under.
   - (C.) The apple seeds fall into the soil hoping to germinate to produce apple trees.
   - D. The little ships are sinking into the quick soil.

Total Problems: Total Correct: Score:

Name ______________________ **Finding Context Clues**

Read the passage. As you consider the meanings of the words in bold, pay close attention to the other words (clues) that surround the bold words. Choose a word from the word box to replace each bold word and write it in the blank provided.

The Life of a Soda Bottle

When I was born, my mother never held me, except for when she shook me to see if my head was on straight. If my head wasn't on straight, she said that I would be considered flat and no one would want me.

My machine mother filled me with a sweet, bubbly liquid. But this was for others to enjoy—not me. She taught me about the world outside our little factory. My father told me that the world was very **merciless** and to be careful once I was on my own.

One day I left my safe home and my machine-like parents, and **ventured** into the "cruel" world. I even left my big, **spacious** room to be packed tightly together for a long, long journey.

When we finally reached our **destination**, I started my new life. I had a new home and made some new friends, some whom had traveled with me from my own home. However, one afternoon a lady came along and with one press of a button, I was out of house and home. She was cruel to me.

My dad had said it would be like this. I **presume** I never believed him. The lady twisted my head off and **regenerated** herself with all my insides. Then, when she was finished, there was nothing more left of me. My life was over.

1. presume ___guess___
2. merciless ___cruel___
3. ventured ___traveled___
4. regenerated ___refreshed___
5. destination ___location___
6. spacious ___roomy___

Word Box
cruel
guess
location
roomy
traveled
refreshed

Total Problems: Total Correct: Score:

Name ______________________ **Best Friends**

Read the passage and answer the questions on pages 24-25.

Best Friends

Hannah Roberts has been my best friend since kindergarten. We have been through many experiences together: slumber parties, football games, cheerleading tryouts, and braces. We have watched one another grow into intelligent, witty, and beautiful young women. I consider myself lucky to have her as my best friend.

In the tenth grade we experienced one of our most important milestones together: our sixteenth birthdays! My sixteenth didn't come until six months after Hannah's. Hannah's sixteenth birthday party was a blast. Her parents surprised her with a car—not a new one, but one that looked almost new. Immediately, she began describing all the places we would go and all the things we could do, now that she had a car. I was just as excited as she was, thinking of all the fun we would have together. It didn't take long for Hannah to get her driver's license. Although my parents were reluctant to let me ride with Hannah alone, eventually they gave in and decided it would be all right.

Our first long-distance driving trip was to the mall, only twenty-five miles from our small town of Manchester, a route I could easily trace in my sleep. That night as I waited for Hannah to pick me up, I began to feel incredibly independent. My parents were finally trusting me, and it felt good. Of course, when Hannah arrived, they still did what I expected, lecturing us on car safety, traffic signals, passing other cars, and intoxicated drivers.

Hannah's driving was safe, and she obeyed all the traffic laws, never attempting to speed or show off. On the way, we discussed our dreams and goals and how we were growing up. She seemed to be so sentimental as we drove along.

After shopping for a long time at the mall, we ate dinner at an Italian restaurant and headed home. It was later than we thought, so we called our parents from my cellular phone to let them know we were safe. We were about five miles from home when a car pulled out in front of us. Hannah pressed hard on the brakes with her foot, but we were too close. We slammed into the side of the car.

The next thing I remember is waking up with a bandaged arm in Rockford emergency room. In the same room lay a man with injuries to the head and arm. I had no sense of what was going on, and looking around, I noticed that Hannah was not in the room. A nurse, a couple of feet away from me, noticed I was awake and called my parents. The three of them were beside me almost immediately. They explained to me that Hannah was hurt very badly. The doctors said she would heal eventually, but it was going to take a long time.

Many months have passed since that horrific night. Hannah is progressing slowly. I visit her every day after school to bolster her spirits and help her catch up with schoolwork. Although the car accident was tragic, Hannah and I have grown closer. I got my driver's license today. I cannot wait for Hannah to get well so that I can drive her to the mall.

Name ______________________ **Best Friends**

Read each question. Circle the letter beside the correct answer where appropriate.

1. The story is mainly about:
   - A. two best friends that get in a car accident
   - B. getting braces
   - C. driving a car on your own for the first time
   - (D) learning to accept yourself
2. Number the sentences in the order in which they occurred in the story.
   - _4_ The girls ate at an Italian restaurant.
   - _1_ Hannah turned sixteen.
   - _6_ The narrator visited Hannah every day after school.
   - _2_ The narrator got her driver's license.
   - _5_ The narrator woke up in the emergency room.
   - _3_ The girls drove to the mall.
3. "Many months have passed since that horrific night." In this sentence from the story, "horrific" means:
   - A. wonderful
   - B. memorable
   - C. stormy
   - (D.) horrible
4. Someone who is laughing "hysterically" is someone who:
   - A. has a medical problem
   - (B.) is laughing uncontrollably
   - C. has permanent hiccups
   - D. makes fun of people who laugh
5. In what town do the girls live?
   - (A) Manchester
   - B. Chattanooga
   - C. Rockford
   - D. New York

Total Problems: Total Correct: Score:

Name ______________________ **Best Friends**

Read each question. Circle the letter beside each correct answer.

6. According to the passage, the girls experienced all of the following together except:
- A. going to college
- B. turning sixteen
- C. cheerleading tryouts
- D. braces

7. Which of the following words is a synonym for "milestone"?
- A. granite
- B. speedometer
- C. brick
- D. benchmark

8. Which of the following is false?
- A. The girls called their parents to tell them they would be late.
- B. The girls had been friends since kindergarten.
- C. The girls ate dinner at an Italian restaurant.
- D. Hannah drove recklessly to the mall.

9. What did Hannah receive from her parents for her birthday?
- A. a computer
- B. a car
- C. a camera
- D. concert tickets

10. Why might the narrator's parents have lectured the girls on driving safely?
- A. They didn't want the girls to have any fun.
- B. They thought Hannah's car had faulty brakes.
- C. Hannah was a new driver.
- D. They were cruel and liked to yell.

11. Who was in the emergency room when the narrator awoke?
- A. Hannah, the nurse, and Hannah's parents
- B. the narrator's parents, an injured man, and the nurse
- C. Hannah and an injured man
- D. Hannah's parents, the narrator's parents, and the nurse

Total Problems: **Total Correct:** **Score:**

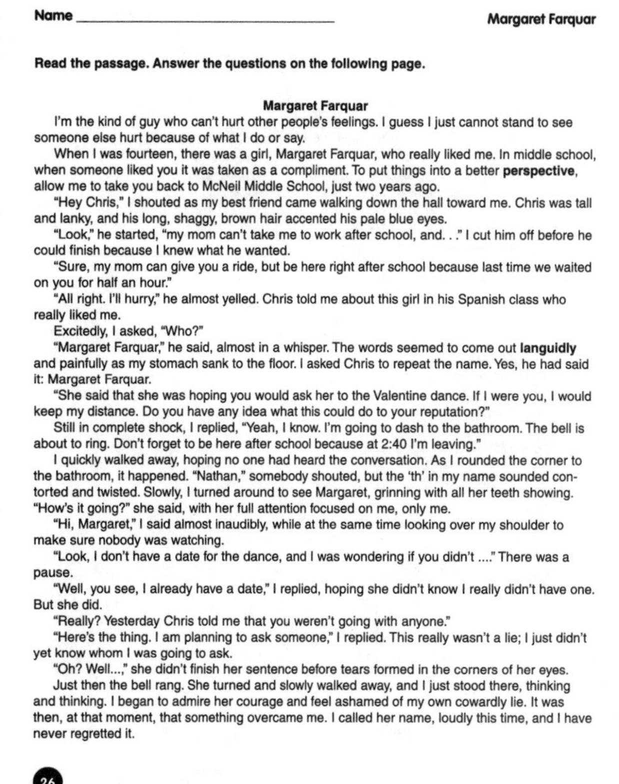

Name ______________________ **Margaret Farquar**

Read the passage. Answer the questions on the following page.

Margaret Farquar

I'm the kind of guy who can't hurt other people's feelings. I guess I just cannot stand to see someone else hurt because of what I do or say.

When I was fourteen, there was a girl, Margaret Farquar, who really liked me. In middle school, when someone liked you it was taken as a compliment. To put things into a better **perspective**, allow me to take you back to McNeil Middle School, just two years ago.

"Hey Chris," I shouted as my best friend came walking down the hall toward me. Chris was tall and lanky, and his long, shaggy, brown hair accented his pale blue eyes.

"Look," he started, "my mom can't take me to work after school, and. . ." I cut him off before he could finish because I knew what he wanted.

"Sure, my mom can give you a ride, but be here right after school because last time we waited on you for half an hour."

"All right. I'll hurry," he almost yelled. Chris told me about this girl in his Spanish class who really liked me.

Excitedly, I asked, "Who?"

"Margaret Farquar," he said, almost in a whisper. The words seemed to come out **languidly** and painfully as my stomach sank to the floor. I asked Chris to repeat the name. Yes, he had said it: Margaret Farquar.

"She said that she was hoping you would ask her to the Valentine dance. If I were you, I would keep my distance. Do you have any idea what this could do to your reputation?"

Still in complete shock, I replied, "Yeah, I know. I'm going to dash to the bathroom. The bell is about to ring. Don't forget to be here after school because at 2:40 I'm leaving."

I quickly walked away, hoping no one had heard the conversation. As I rounded the corner to the bathroom, it happened. "Nathan," somebody shouted, but the 'th' in my name sounded contorted and twisted. Slowly, I turned around to see Margaret, grinning with all her teeth showing. "How's it going?" she said, with her full attention focused on me, only me.

"Hi, Margaret," I said almost inaudibly, while at the same time looking over my shoulder to make sure nobody was watching.

"Look, I don't have a date for the dance, and I was wondering if you didn't ...." There was a pause.

"Well, you see, I already have a date," I replied, hoping she didn't know I really didn't have one. But she did.

"Really? Yesterday Chris told me that you weren't going with anyone."

"Here's the thing. I am planning to ask someone," I replied. This really wasn't a lie; I just didn't yet know whom I was going to ask.

"Oh? Well...," she didn't finish her sentence before tears formed in the corners of her eyes.

Just then the bell rang. She turned and slowly walked away, and I just stood there, thinking and thinking. I began to admire her courage and feel ashamed of my own cowardly lie. It was then, at that moment, that something overcame me. I called her name, loudly this time, and I have never regretted it.

Name ______________________ **Margaret Farquar**

Read each question. Circle the letter beside each correct answer.

1. Referring to: "The words seemed to come out languidly,"—the word "languidly" means:
- A. slowly
- B. quickly
- C. lively
- D. briskly

2. The main idea of the story is that:
- A. High school is a stressful time for all teenagers.
- B. No one should be made to feel humiliated because of who he is.
- C. The Valentine dance is a big event, but not everyone is able to attend.
- D. Friends cannot always be trusted.

3. In the last paragraph, the narrator says "something overcame me." What inference is implied here, based on reading the entire story?
- A. Margaret should not have approached him so aggressively.
- B. The narrator should have listened more closely to Chris's advice.
- C. The narrator realized that he should not ask Margaret to the dance.
- D. The narrator feels badly that he is "responsible" for Margaret's tears and sadness.

4. All the following describe Chris except:
- A. pale blue eyes
- B. tall and lanky
- C. short, blond hair
- D. best friend

5. Which one of the following statements is false?
- A. The name of the school is McNeil Middle School.
- B. The narrator was fifteen when Margaret liked him.
- C. The name of the narrator is Nathan.
- D. Margaret was in Chris's Spanish class.

Total Problems: **Total Correct:** **Score:**

Name ______________________ **The Corn Patch Ghost**

Read the passage and answer the questions on the following page.

The Corn Patch Ghost

There is a true story that my grandmother tells, and whenever she tells it, everyone has a good laugh, everyone except my great-grandfather. The story takes place a long time ago, back in the early 1900s in a rural area.

It was the second time that month that he had been out way past dark. The kids were distressed, especially Shirley, who repeated "Daddy is still not home, Mama." Shirley was the most fervent of the six children, and she loved Daddy very much.

"Don't you worry, Shirley. I'll make sure he will be home tomorrow night," Mama guaranteed. From the look on Mama's face, we could tell she was up to something. We would just have to wait and see.

As we sat down for supper, each in his or her own place, my oldest brother asked if he should ask the blessing. "Go ahead, son," said Mama, eyeing the empty seat directly across from hers.

After supper I helped to put the two young babies to bed and started on my schoolwork, while Henry and Agnes washed the dishes and cleaned the kitchen. "Where is Mama?" I asked my older sister Lee.

"Well, I don't know," replied Lee, "Maybe she went to the barn."

I was a little baffled; it wasn't like Mama to leave the house after dark, but on the other hand, she was not the type to explain herself to anyone. I finished my schoolwork, prepared for bed, and read a bedtime story to Tina, my younger sister who had just begun school this year.

"I hope Mama is safe," I said nervously to Lee before retiring to bed.

"I'm almost positive she is just fine," Lee said half assuringly. She didn't sound too sure of herself, but she was trying to be the grown-up in the house. Then, she rushed the rest of us off to bed. Lee and I shared a bed, and I was exceptionally glad that night.

"I hope Mama gets back soon," I said worriedly as Lee and I **crouched** under the covers. "It is really chilly out." Lee just nodded her head, and I began to drift into a fitful sleep when a scream roused me out of bed. Quickly, Lee and I ran to the window to get a look at the disturbance outside. Just as I raised the window shade, the front door burst open and Daddy, out of breath and white as a sheet, entered the house. By then, Lee and I were in the front room witnessing my daddy's state of being. Lee yelled, "What's going on?"

"Ghost!" he tried to whisper. "A ghost in the corn patch! It chased me all the way to the house!" He certainly looked as if he had seen a ghost, but it didn't take Lee and me long to realize that Daddy had again stopped at Uncle Fred's for a little swig of moonshine. "Quick, girls, get into bed, and don't make a sound," he instructed us. We did as he said, and shortly thereafter we heard the front door open again. We began to piece together the puzzle and had a great laugh.

Early the next morning, Mama was there to get all of us out of bed. As Lee and I were warming by the fire, Mama winked and pulled a white sheet from under the couch as she casually told us that Daddy would not be missing any more suppers for awhile. Then Lee said, "I guess Daddy really did see a ghost."

Name ______________________ **The Corn Patch Ghost**

Read each question. Circle the letter beside each correct answer.

1. Referring to the last paragraph when Mama "winked and pulled a white sheet from under the couch," one might possibly conclude that:
- A. Mama had hidden Daddy's favorite white sheet under the couch.
- B. Mama was planning to do something with the white sheet.
- (C) Mama was the ghost in the corn patch that scared Daddy.
- D. Mama was planning to give Daddy a new white sheet.

2. A synonym for the word "fervent" is:
- (A) impassioned
- B. sleepy
- C. smart
- D. athletic

3. In the tenth paragraph, what are the context clues for the meaning of the word "roused"?
- A. fitful sleep
- (B) awakened
- C. drift
- D. began

4. All of the following are true except:
- A. Tina had just begun school.
- B. Lee and the narrator shared a bed for sleeping.
- (C) Daddy had been at Uncle Frankie's drinking moonshine.
- D. Shirley was the emotional child in the family.

© Carson-Dellosa CD-2207 | **Total Problems:** | **Total Correct:** | **Score:** | 29

Name ______________________ **Losing Touch**

Read the passage and answer the questions on the following page.

Losing Touch

The farm was ready for slumber, and he could finally sit down and think. He desperately needed to think. Lately, he was having so much trouble trying to remember. Settling into his worn chair, he gazed out the window and slipped into a deep meditation. He owned a farm. He had a wife. He called her Darling.

Darling...where was she? Oh, yes, there she was in the kitchen preparing a meal. He could hear her. He had three sons and a daughter. And where were they? He glanced at the clock. They should have been home from school hours ago. He became agitated as he listened for their childish voices to penetrate the fog covering his mind. No...nothing.

He slowly rose and walked into the kitchen. He asked Darling where the children were. She turned to him with her sweet smile, but the smile quickly faded when she noticed he wasn't jesting. She quietly explained to him that the children were grown now and had families of their own. Puzzled, he sat down. Yes, this was true. He remembered now; Darling had told him this yesterday. He smiled at her before pulling her into his arms.

"I love you, Darling. I promise I will never forget you," he told her. A tear slipped from her big green eyes, and he kissed it away. She smiled then and they sat down to dinner. He had been so nervous lately. Later, they went into the living room where he got out their picture albums and requested that she go over the pictures with him, just so he wouldn't forget. As he looked at the pictures, **immersed** in naming all the people in the pictures and the places they had traveled, she looked at him sadly. She nodded as he repeated every name correctly. Gently, she took his hand. He was slipping from her every day, though he struggled against it. She knew not how, only that he was slowly losing touch with their perfect world. Once, when he glanced up and grinned at her, she was lost in his deep blue eyes.

The days and nights became repetitious. He found it too difficult sometimes. He was awakened suddenly from his slumber. Wiping the sweat from his brow, he crept from their bed, careful not to awaken Darling. He needed to think. He walked to the window and gazed at the orange moon. He owned a farm. He had a wife. He called her Darling. He had three sons and a daughter. Where were they? Oh, yes...with their families. He sighed in relief. He remembered. He was fine.

Many nights he awoke, frantic to remember. He paced around the room straining to remember. There was his farm, his Darling, his sons, and a daughter.

"What is wrong?" Darling would ask him.

"I'm just nervous, Darling, go back to sleep."

One evening as she called him to supper the third time, she knew something was wrong. She found him at his desk. Walking quietly behind him, she saw he was desperately writing the names of his family. As she turned and silently left the room, tears streamed down her face, and she knew he was going to leave her. His mind was becoming too cluttered to remember.

30 © Carson-Dellosa CD-2207

Name ______________________ **Losing Touch**

Read each question. Circle the letter beside each correct answer.

1. One might conclude that since the old man is having trouble remembering events and people, he might be experiencing the symptoms of:
- A. cancer
- B. tuberculosis
- (C) Alzheimer's
- D. malaria

2. In the fourth paragraph, what is another word that means "immersed"?
- A. daydreamed
- (B) absorbed
- C. unabsorbed
- D. fantasized

3. Which one of the following is not true about the man's family?
- A. The children are grown and have families of their own.
- B. He lives on a farm with Darling, his wife.
- C. Sometimes he remembered events, and sometimes he did not.
- (D) He had two sons and a daughter.

4. "The days and nights became repetitious. He found it too difficult sometimes. He was awakened suddenly from his slumber." What are the context clues for the meaning of "slumber"?
- A. became repetitious
- B. days and nights
- (C) awakened from
- D. too difficult

5. Referring to the fourth paragraph and the sentence, "Once, when he glanced up and grinned at her, she was lost in his deep blue eyes," one could infer that:
- (A) She is still very much in love with her husband.
- B. She is trying to analyze and assess her husband's illness.
- C. She has the same illness as he.
- D. She was confused by what he was saying and doing.

© Carson-Dellosa CD-2207 | **Total Problems:** | **Total Correct:** | **Score:** | 31

Name ______________________ **Mallory's Big Splash**

Read the passage and answer the questions on the following page.

Mallory's Big Splash

Summer is a favorite time of the year for my family. For me, summer means rest and relaxation from the busy school year. For Mallory and Trey, my younger sister and brother, summer means independence. The three of us have grown up on a farm, which has instilled in us a strong sense of independence. During the summer, Mallory and Trey are able to come and go as they please, as long as they do not wander off the farm and get into any trouble.

A few summers ago on a typical hot July day, Mallory and Trey were carelessly riding their bicycles and sporting about in the pasture. Feeling restless, they decided to race their bikes down to the pond to catch frogs, bugs, and snakes. Mallory was in the lead, but Trey was close behind. As Mallory approached the pond, a swarm of gnats overcame her and temporarily blinded her. With her bike still moving and her eyes closed, she sailed off the **embankment** that surrounded the pond, and into the murky water with a big splash.

Trey arrived at the pond a few seconds later. He recounts a scene he will never forget. Mallory was standing up to her waist in muddy water with green pond algae limply hanging from her head and arms. Instead of immediately going to her rescue, Trey just stood there gawking and teasing her as some bratty little brothers would. Furthermore, he quickly ran home to share Mallory's **humiliation** with Mom. He just knew, and hoped, that Mallory would get into trouble for not watching where she was going.

As Trey was trying to explain to Mom what had happened, Mallory, dripping wet with green algae all over her body, knocked on the back door. When Mom went to the door, all she could do was laugh and laugh. Mom later said that Mallory looked like a little swamp monster from some movie, and she didn't smell too good either.

Trey had hoped Mallory would receive some kind of punishment because he was that type of brother. Mom thought Mallory's ordeal was punishment enough, and so did I. However, to this day our family still has a big laugh whenever the story of Mallory's big splash is retold.

32 © Carson-Dellosa CD-2207

Name ______________________ **Mallory's Big Splash**

Read each question. Circle the letter beside each correct answer.

1. What caused Mallory to plunge into the murky pond?
   A. She was not watching very closely as she rode her bike.
   B. Trey purposely pushed her into the water.
   (C.) A swarm of gnats overcame her and temporarily blinded her.
   D. She was trying to get away from a raging bull.
2. An antonym for the word "humiliation" is:
   A. anger
   (B.) praise
   C. downgrading
   D. embarrassment
3. Which one of the following events happened first?
   A. Mallory, dripping wet with green algae all over her body, knocked on the door.
   B. He quickly ran home to share Mallory's humiliation with Mom.
   (C.) They decided to race their bikes down to the pond to catch frogs, bugs, and snakes.
   D. She sailed off the embankment that surrounded the pond, and into the murky water.
4. Referring to the following sentences taken from the third paragraph, "Trey arrived at the pond a few seconds later. He recounts a scene he will never forget,"—what are the context clues for the word "recounts"?
   A. at the pond
   B. never forget
   (C.) a scene
   D. a few seconds later
5. When Mother saw Mallory standing in the doorway, she said Mallory looked like:
   A. a frog
   B. brown, murky water
   C. green algae
   (D.) a little swamp monster
6. What is the setting of the story?
   A. a school
   B. a bank
   (C.) a farm
   D. a kitchen
7. Referring to the phrase, "she sailed off the embankment,"—"embankment" means a:
   (A.) slope
   B. straight road
   C. river
   D. narrow bridge

Total Problems: Total Correct: Score:

Name ______________________ **The Parachute**

Read the passage and answer the questions on the following page.

The Parachute

Bruner Ray Fortenberry is such a wonderful name for a cat. At least, I think so. Bruner was such a fun cat, and he brought many good times and memories to my family and me. Playful and **nimble**, Bruner loved to hide and tangle with boxes. My Aunt Sammi always enjoyed spinning him in a box until he would jump out and lay crouched on the floor as if he were stalking the box. He would remain in this position until something else diverted his attention. He could go on like this for hours at a time, as long as someone was willing to play with him.

Bruner also loved to play with paper bags. During Christmas vacation one year, Bruner was playing in a grocery bag while I was emptying the trash. As I was putting a new trash bag into the can, I realized that Bruner had just about had a coronary. He really hated the sound of trash bags. In fact, this startled him so badly that he shot out of the kitchen like lightning. However, somehow during his great endeavor to get away, he managed to wrap a grocery bag around his neck and stomach. At that moment, all I could think about was the Christmas tree. I was just hoping that he would not destroy the tree while trying to get out of what he thought was harm's way.

Considering Bruner was running as fast as a bullet, I could not see how he could possibly miss the tree. Contrary to my beliefs, he managed to dodge the tree, but he did run directly into the piano. This scene happened so quickly I did not know how to react. He seemed so pitiful and awestruck that I just wanted to hold him. Even though he was still wrapped in the grocery bag, he appeared to be okay because he was still jumping and trying to untangle himself. When I realized he was not hurt, I began laughing. Replaying the scene in my mind, I sat on the floor and laughed. This jocund cat! Again, Bruner became startled, and he took off running just as he did the first time. That was when I realized that the bag on his back looked like a parachute.

Bruner recently became very sick and had to be put to sleep. Sometimes, I think about him and feel sad, but then I think about his "parachute" incident and laugh. Even though he is not with me anymore, he left me with some lasting memories.

Name ______________________ **The Parachute**

Read each question. Circle the letter beside each correct answer.

1. "Playful and *nimble*, Bruner loved to hide and tangle with boxes." "Nimble" means:
   (A.) quick
   B. funny
   C. easy
   D. afraid
2. The main idea is:
   A. Don't allow your pet to play with cardboard boxes.
   B. Pets can be clumsy and hazardous if allowed to play in the house.
   C. Be careful when you permit pets near Christmas trees.
   (D.) Pets can provide happy memories.
3. Which one of the following events happened last in the story?
   (A.) He appeared to be okay because he was still jumping and trying to untangle himself.
   B. Bruner was playing in a grocery bag while I was emptying the trash.
   C. He managed to wrap a grocery bag. . .around his neck and stomach.
   D. My Aunt Sammi always enjoyed spinning him in a box.
4. Read the fourth paragraph and especially the following sentence: "When I realized he was not hurt, I began laughing. Replaying the scene in my mind, I sat on the floor and laughed. This jocund cat!" What is a context clue for the word "jocund"?
   A. replaying
   B. lay
   (C.) laughed
   D. hurt
5. Where does the title of the story originate?
   A. Wearing a parachute once, Bruner jumped out of a plane.
   (B.) Bruner looked like he was wearing a parachute when he was running with a bag wrapped around him.
   C. Bruner is big and round as a parachute.
   D. Bruner became entangled in a parachute and could not see where he was running.

Total Problems: Total Correct: Score:

Name ______________________ **The Lunar Danger**

Read the passage and answer the questions on the following page.

The Lunar Danger

The view from the Fifth Lunar Observatory was breathtaking. The stars shine brighter there than on Earth. Without a true atmosphere, the Earth's moon is a great location for a celestial observatory. My name is Michael, and I worked aboard the observatory, built in 2112, located just south of the Tsiolkovsky Crater. This was an ideal location because most of the time the main telescope faced away from the sun. We enjoyed an **unobstructed** view of the heavens but the spacecraft had to shield us from temperatures nearing –200°F.

My usual workday consisted of maneuvering the main telescope, Hubble IV, which was the descendent of the original Hubble telescope. I had an assistant, Robert, to help me. Every morning we received coordinates of a star, constellation, or planet that interested scientists on Earth.

On November 7, 2113, Robert and I received orders to focus the telescope on the constellation Gemini. According to the report we received, scientists had picked up electromagnetic activity near Gemini. Robert and I began entering the data into the computer and focusing the telescope. As the Hubble IV was rotating in the direction of Gemini, the main motor started smoking. I yelled at Robert to turn off the machine. By the time he pressed the last button, the main observation room had filled with smoke. That was the least of our problems; the electrical fire had also knocked out our main power.

Luckily, the emergency lights came on, but our temperature control unit was severely damaged. Without the TCU, a stable temperature of 72°F could not be maintained in the lunar complex. I estimated we had only ninety minutes before we would freeze.

Robert reminded me of an escape rover in one of the cargo bays. Where would we go, though? The nearest settlement was the Fourth Lunar Observatory, but it had been closed for six years. Our situation worsened by the minute. I watched the temperature on the thermometer drop every minute. We couldn't contact anyone since we were on the far side of the moon. The temperature was down to 54°, and I was feeling sick. This looked like the end.

As I was trying to keep warm, I glanced at Robert's watch. It was then 4:05 P.M. Suddenly, I was overwhelmed with joy. The lunar sunrise was to take place at 4:08 P.M. With the sun's rays shining directly on us, we would begin to warm. Although the outside temperature could reach 250°F, we would have plenty of time to start the cooling system manually. Using the outside solar panels for energy, we successfully started the cooling system.

However, our troubles were not over yet. Soon the sun would go down, and we would surely freeze to death. However, we were able to contact the new international space station and request that Earth send down a rescue ship and pick us up. On our way home, I began to look forward to the relatively stable temperatures of planet Earth.

Name ______________________________ **The Lunar Danger**

Read each question. Circle the letter beside each correct answer.

1. Who rescued Robert and the narrator?
   A. Gemini voyager
   B. Sixth Lunar Observatory
   C. Challenger
   (D.) people from the international space station
2. An inference one could make after reading the story is that:
   A. Electromagnetic activity should be studied more closely.
   (B.) Life outside Earth is difficult to maintain.
   C. Human beings should not attempt to live outside of Earth.
   D. There are some planets near Earth with human life.
3. What was the cause of the accident that eventually sent Robert and the narrator home to Earth?
   A. attack from Gemini
   B. lightning storm
   (C.) electrical fire
   D. electromagnetic activity
4. A word that means the opposite of "unobstructed" is:
   A. non-interference
   B. unimpede
   (C.) blocked
   D. view
5. The temperature outside the observatory could reach as high as:
   A. 200°F
   (B.) 250°F
   C. –250°F
   D. 72°F

Total Problems:	Total Correct:	Score:

Name ______________________________ **Sweet Sixteen**

Read the passage and answer the questions on the following page.

Sweet Sixteen

Staying with a friend while my mother and stepfather were out of town, I woke up at a strange house with one of those familiar bad feelings in my stomach. I was sixteen today, but that didn't mean much to me for some reason.

Recently, I had decided to leave my mother to live with my father and stepmother in Alabama because my stepfather and I got along as well as the coyote and the roadrunner. Perhaps this is a bit of an overstatement concerning our relationship, but still, I was moving.

After breakfast, Jackie convinced me that I should visit our other friend, Kate. She had a big swimming pool, but today swimming didn't seem so exciting. To make Jackie and Kate happy, I decided to oblige and visit Kate. However, this feeling in my stomach had been tenacious since the day I decided to leave and live with my father in Alabama. But today, for my friends, I tried to look as if I were enjoying myself.

After a long drive, we finally pulled into Kate's driveway. When I knocked on the door, Kate answered and immediately ordered me to shut my eyes because she had a surprise for me. As Kate led me around the yard, I imagined a birthday present that I probably would hate but would have to pretend to like.

After a few minutes of sensing that we were walking around the house to the back, Kate finally allowed me to open my eyes. I was facing the swimming pool, and every person I had cared about at all since the day I moved to Atlanta was there at the pool, yelling "Surprise!" For a split second, I did not quite know how to react or what to say, and it felt like my heart stopped beating for a few seconds.

That day took away the dire feeling in my stomach, and I have never had that feeling again. The realization that even after I moved away my friends would still be there for me made me a stronger person. I was strong enough after that day to leave and begin a new life because I knew that no matter what happened, my friends would always be there for me.

My sweet sixteen birthday turned out to be the best birthday yet, and the new friends I have made here in Alabama will undoubtedly make my next birthday even better.

Name ______________________________ **Sweet Sixteen**

Read each question. Circle the letter beside each correct answer.

1. The story is mainly about:
   A. a swimming party
   (B.) friendship
   C. an unfair stepfather
   D. a sixteenth birthday
2. Referring to: "However, this feeling in my stomach had been tenacious since the day I decided to leave and live with my father in Alabama,"—the context clues for the meaning of the word "tenacious" are:
   A. in my stomach
   B. to leave and live
   C. I decided
   (D.) feeling in my stomach
3. Which one of the following statements is not true?
   A. Kate answered and immediately ordered me to shut my eyes because she had a surprise for me.
   B. She convinced me that I should visit our other friend Kate.
   (C.) Every person I cared about at all since the day I moved to Alabama was there.
   D. I had decided to leave my mother to live with my father and stepmother.
4. A synonym for the word "dire" is:
   A. nauseous
   B. empty
   (C.) horrible
   D. guilty
5. Which of the following statements is a conclusion one might draw from reading the story?
   (A.) Life is easier if one has good friends on whom to depend.
   B. One should accept a stepparent, regardless of differences of opinion.
   C. Birthday parties for sixteen-year-olds are the best in Atlanta.
   D. Don't count on your friends to be there when you need them.

Total Problems:	Total Correct:	Score:

Name ______________________________ **Refuse Fear**

Read the passage and answer the questions on the following page.

Refuse Fear

During the summer between my eighth- and ninth-grade years, I went to Maui, Hawaii, on a vacation with my family. Since I had never been to Hawaii, I decided I wanted to do all I could to enjoy myself. There were many exciting activities, including scuba diving, biking, surfing, and parasailing. Since I tended to be afraid of heights and deep water, I decided to engage in parasailing in order to overcome this fear.

When we arrived at the beach, our coordinator told us that the boat was malfunctioning, so we would have to wait until another boat was ready. This waiting did not help my nerves one bit. I kept thinking this was a sign for me to back out. I tried to calm my nerves by swimming and playing on the beach with my sister.

The wait was only about one hour, and then we were on our way. The little motor-powered raft transported us to the main boat sitting out in the water. I thought my nerves had calmed until I stepped onto the main boat, and then I almost panicked. I said to my family that I could not do it by myself. Thankfully, my sister Celina agreed to go up with me.

In no time, we were in the bay, and everyone was putting on harnesses and life vests. All of a sudden, I felt faint and began to turn white. In fact, I do not know how I remained on my feet. In the meantime, our boat was speeding along at 50 mph, and we were told to move to the back of the boat and sit down with our legs extended and arms around a bar.

As the parachute was unhooked, we lifted upward into the air. I was yelling and holding my sister's hand and arm. Once we reached our peak, the air was calm, and for miles I could see our side of the island. I could even see Haleakala Volcano on the other side of the island. The ride was awesome, and after a few seconds I was less nervous and even smiled for a photographer in a not-too-distant helicopter who was taking pictures that we could eventually buy.

The sailing through the air lasted only a short ten minutes. As the boat pretended to drop us where we had begun, we were surprised when the boat accelerated, and once again we were lifted into the wide blue. Being more alert and not so scared this time, I could look down into the water beneath me. My sister and I did see, we thought, two small tiger sharks swimming below us in the water. I certainly was glad I was in the air, not in the water.

Finally, we were dropped onto the beach, and after many thanks and compliments to our boatmen, we left to explore other cool things to do in this paradise away from home. Riding along, I was feeling proud and confident because I had faced two of my fears, and I was ready to tackle the world.

Name ______________________________ Refuse Fear

Read each question. Circle the letter beside each correct answer.

1. The story is mainly about:
   A. a young girl who learns to parasail in Hawaii
   B. all the fun activities to do on vacation in Hawaii
   C. two sisters bonding on a vacation in Hawaii
   (D) building self-confidence and refusing fear
2. Referring to the sentence, "When we arrived at the beach, our coordinator told us that the boat was malfunctioning, so we would have to wait until another boat was ready,"—what are the context clues for the word "malfunctioning"?
   (A) wait, another boat
   B. we would have
   C. arrived at the beach
   D. coordinator told us
3. An antonym for the word "alleviate" is:
   A. lessen
   B. relieve
   (C) worsen
   D. stop
4. With whom does the speaker in the story share her vacation?
   A. sister
   (B) family
   C. sister and brother
   D. no one
5. A conclusion one might draw after reading the story is that:
   A. The narrator will never want to parasail again.
   B. Hawaii is the right place to vacation if one wants a variety of activities.
   (C) The narrator will be more successful in life because she is learning self-confidence.
   D. The narrator will become more difficult for her parents to handle.
6. Which one of the following events happened last?
   A. I tried to calm my nerves by swimming and playing on the beach.
   (B) We left to explore other cool things to do in this paradise.
   C. I was yelling and holding my sister's hand and arm.
   D. My sister and I did see two small tiger sharks swimming below us in the water.

Total Problems: Total Correct: Score:

Name ______________________________ Slippery Stairs

Read the passage and answer the questions on the following page.

Slippery Stairs

Wood can be very pretty in a home. It can be used for almost everything: tables, floors, desks, chairs, or in my case, stairs. To keep wood clean, one has to clean and polish it often. This is where my story begins.

One night, as my mom and dad were leaving to go to the mall, they left instructions for me to clean and polish the stairs. The words "clean" and "polish" are still debated—even today.

I am the type of person who doesn't mind hard work, so I grabbed a broom and first swept the stairs. I have always enjoyed being told that I have done a good job, so that night I wanted to do a good job. Therefore, I was determined to make the old wooden stairs look new again. I must have spent two hours rubbing and polishing the steps over and over again, as I listened to Spanish CDs. I am in my third year of Spanish at Rockwell Middle School, and that night I thought I could accomplish two things at once. You know—two birds with one stone.

When my parents arrived home around 9:00 that night, they promptly noticed the stairs and were terribly impressed with how they were shining. After thanking me and beginning to ascend the steps, my parents said good-night as I retreated to the den where I had been watching a movie. I had just sat down when I heard a yelp and a series of thuds coming from the direction of the stairs. Running into the living room, I saw my dad lying at the bottom of the stairs.

My dad had slipped on the stairs and had made a thunderous acrobatic tumble to the bottom. Of course, my first impulse was to burst into laughter since he appeared to be unhurt, but I didn't. The mental image of my dad rolling down the stairs made self-control almost impossible as I attempted to help him to his feet.

Once he was on his feet and had regained feeling in his whole body, he began to laugh, and I joined him. However, it was our laughing that brought my mom onto the scene, since she had not heard the series of thuds. When she realized what had happened, she was furious with me and scolded me for polishing the stairs. She said someone could have been seriously hurt, and I should have known better. I told her I did what I thought I was told to do. She insisted she never told me to polish the stairs and that I had misunderstood.

During the next week, there were a few other minor falls. My dad especially was very careful on the stairs. One night, just to irritate my mom, my dad threw a heavy cardboard box down the stairs to **simulate** his fall. Thinking my dad had once again fallen, my mom ran to the stairs, only to find the box at the bottom and my dad at the top of the stairs, waving and yelling. It was hilarious; at least, my dad and I thought so.

Name ______________________________ Slippery Stairs

Read each question. Circle the letter beside each correct answer.

1. The main idea of the story is:
   A. Stairs need to be cleaned and polished regularly.
   (B) Misunderstandings can sometimes be humorous.
   C. Parents can sometimes be wrong.
   D. Chores can be entertaining.
2. Another word for "simulate" is:
   A. different B. add
   C. initiate (D) imitate
3. Which one of the following statements is not true?
   (A) I listened to French CDs.
   B. She was furious with me and scolded me for polishing the stairs.
   C. My first impulse was to burst into laughter since he appeared to be unhurt.
   D. The words "polish" and "clean" are still debated, even today.
4. Which one of the following events happened first?
   A. My dad threw a cardboard box down the stairs to simulate his fall down the stairs.
   B. I had just sat down when I heard a yelp and a series of thuds.
   C. It was our laughing that brought my mom onto the scene.
   (D) They left instructions for me to clean and polish the stairs.
5. Where were the speaker's parents when the speaker cleaned and polished the stairs?
   A. in the den
   (B) at the mall
   C. at a PTA meeting
   D. at a business meeting
6. Which one of the following words was the basis for the conflict in the story?
   (A) polish
   B. thuds
   C. stairs
   D. broom
7. Which one of the following words does not describe the speaker?
   A. hard worker
   B. determined
   (C) lazy
   D. industrious

Total Problems: Total Correct: Score:

Name ______________________________ The Mud Puppy

Read the passage and answer the questions on the folowing page.

The Mud Puppy

Last summer, two of my friends and I got the urge to fish at Guntersville Lake. Since this was the first summer that we were old enough to drive, we thought this would be something new and fun to do. Furthermore, the lake is quite large, sprawling around the whole city, and walking around with a tackle box and a rod would take too much time and would be too cumbersome. Therefore, we decided that it would be in our best interest to bring a fishing boat with us.

Since I had always enjoyed fishing and was hoping to learn how to duck hunt, the idea of being able to fish anywhere on the lake was just about the best thing I could imagine. I had been fishing out of an old, leaky aluminum boat in our cow pond. The boat was still in fair condition, I thought, so my friends and I attempted to make it "seaworthy." The blissful thought of fishing on the lake in a decent boat must have clouded our judgment. After a coat of paint, a new transom, and an attempt to stop the leaking rivets, we realized that she was beyond repair.

Disappointed but not beaten, we diligently searched to find a suitable boat. Occupying all our free moments, the search became an obsession. If the search were not punishment enough, we were often teased by finding a boat that seemed to meet our meager requirements, only to find it lacking in some major area or two. The trailer would be missing, or it would be two hundred dollars too expensive. On one occasion, we called with intention to purchase, only to learn that the boat had already been sold. However, just when we thought that we should give up on the boat, things changed.

Chad, one of my friends, spotted a boat in a nearby neighbor's yard. The boat was a fourteen-foot long, flat-bottomed, deep-hulled boat, complete with a trailer. It wasn't in mint condition, but I could see potential right away. Getting her back to operating condition would be a big job, but it could and would be done if the owner would sell her.

Initially, my two friends and I had agreed to a three-way partnership in the boat if we found one. However, my friends' funds were almost **depleted**, and if the boat were to be bought, I would be the one to do it.

Soon after Chad had told me about the boat, I stopped by the house to inquire. The old man who owned the boat said he hadn't used it in twenty years and would be happy just to get it out of his yard. I asked him how much he would take for the boat, and he replied that I could just take it. It was free!

Once home, I quickly began work on my "new" boat. She needed a transom, a good wire brushing, two new trailer tires, a paint job, and lights. But most importantly, she needed a motor, which I finally found after searching the classifieds. After a few weeks of hard work and a little money, she was ready for the water. However, she did need one more important thing: a name. Since the boat was small and slow, an intimidating name wouldn't be right. I would be using it for fishing and duck hunting, so she would be operating in some mud and muck. Therefore, the only name I thought fitting was "The Mud Puppy."

Name ______________________ **The Mud Puppy**

Read each question. Circle the letter beside each correct answer.

1. "The Mud Puppy" is the name of a:
   A. little dirty puppy
   B. car
   C. brown guppy
   D. boat

2. The main idea of the story is:
   A. Fishing and hunting at Guntersville Lake is fun.
   B. Believing something and then working to obtain it is rewarding.
   C. Finding something to occupy one's time in the summer is important.
   D. Buying a fishing boat is a difficult process.

3. "The old man who owned the boat said he hadn't used it in twenty years and would be happy just to get it out of his yard. I asked him how much he would take for the boat, and he replied that I could just take it. It was free!" After reading the story, one might infer that the old man gave the speaker the boat because:
   A. The boat was stolen and the old man wanted to get rid of it.
   B. The old man was moving away.
   C. The man was getting old, and the boat required many repairs.
   D. The old man's wife insisted he give the boat away.

4. Another word for "depleted" is:
   A. stolen
   B. depended
   C. exhausted
   D. doubled

5. Which one of the following is not what the boat needed?
   A. lights
   B. transom
   C. paint job
   D. kitchen

Total Problems: Total Correct: Score:

Name ______________________ **A Boring Vacation**

Read the passage and answer the questions on the following page.

A Boring Vacation

Sam sighed loudly as he entered the den. He hoped to get his mother's attention by doing this. He was bored, and she always had good ideas for things to do. She didn't wake up, though. He told Andy, his older brother, that he was going bike riding, and he sprinted away.

It was summer, and there wasn't much for a thirteen-year-old to do in rural Mississippi. He was biking down the road, thinking of what to do next, when suddenly he hit a hole and swerved off the road.

"Whoa!" Sam yelled as his bike headed toward a freshly dug ditch. He had managed to pull himself out when he heard something.

"Hey, kid, go away!" yelled a voice from the other side of the road. It appeared to be coming from Blue Creek.

"Who...who's there?" Sam called cautiously.

"None of your business!" yelled the same voice. "Now, beat it before you get yourself hurt!"

Sam swiftly ran to his bike, but before he could leave, a car stopped and yelled at the unseen voice. "You'll be sorry for this!" yelled someone from inside the car.

The car then sped away quickly. Without hesitating, Sam pedaled as fast as his long legs would go. When he arrived home, he threw his bike on the front porch and rushed inside.

"Sam Timon, look at yourself! You're a mess! Now, go clean up and get ready for supper," his mom commanded as he entered the house.

Sam did as his mother said, but he was eager to tell everyone about his adventure. At dinner he explained what had happened. He told about the voice, but no one seemed to care. He cared though, and he was determined to find out who the **enigmatic** voice was at Blue Creek.

The next day, thinking his bike would make too much noise, he hiked to Blue Creek. Shortly after he arrived, he saw two men talking, and he recognized one of the voices as the man he had heard yesterday. Furthermore, he saw shovels lying on the ground beside the two men. He had seen a movie in which two men buried stolen money they had acquired after robbing the local bank. Sam's heart jumped.

Sam listened to the men's conversation. Before he could stop himself, he sneezed, and both men jumped. The man whose voice he had discerned quickly walked in his direction; however, Sam was too scared to move.

"Sorry about the scare I gave you yesterday, kid. We've been digging a ditch here, and we were just about ready to let the water rush in. I just wanted to keep you from getting hurt," the familiar voice said in a pleasant tone.

Feeling a surge of relief overcome his body, Sam was grateful the man had explained everything—almost everything. "What about the car that drove by yesterday and yelled at you?" he asked curiously.

"Oh! That was one of my neighbors. He has tried to stop this ditch all along, but we really do need it. Without it, the creek would overflow and wash the road away," the man explained convincingly. Sam talked a few more minutes with the men and then left for home.

"Now," he thought to himself as he walked along, "it will be a boring vacation." A few minutes later, reflecting on what had happened the past two days, again Sam thought to himself, "Well, maybe, a boring vacation isn't so bad."

Name ______________________ **A Boring Vacation**

Read each question. Circle the letter beside each correct answer.

1. Sam found out that the two men were actually:
   A. hiding money which they had stolen from a bank in town
   B. hiding from the police because they had committed a crime
   C. digging a ditch to prevent the road from washing away
   D. planting trees to help the environmentalists in the local community

2. "Feeling a surge of relief overcome his body, Sam was grateful the man had explained everything—almost everything." What are the context clues that suggest the meaning of the word "grateful"?
   A. overcome, body
   B. explained, his
   C. almost, everything
   D. feeling, surge, relief

3. Which statement is true?
   A. Sam heard a voice that said, "Hey, boy, go away!"
   B. Sam didn't ride his bike to Blue Creek the second day.
   C. The story takes place in rural Missouri.
   D. The first day at Blue Crane, Sam yelled, "Who...who's there?"

Total Problems: Total Correct: Score:

Name ______________________ **An Unusual Day**

Read the passage and answer the questions on the following page.

An Unusual Day

The sun leaked through the tiny cracks in my blinds. The morning sun was shining brightly when I opened my eyes. The room was a pale yellow with tiny chips missing at the edge of the baseboard across from my bed. This was the first night in my new apartment, and I loved it. The apartment building was only three blocks from the bookstore where I worked part-time. The small store housed hundreds of books, new and old. I was in charge of keeping all of them in order. It was a nice job for a full-time student.

One morning as I was casually strolling down the street to work, I happened to bump into an older gentleman. As I was making apologies and attempting to hide my embarrassment, I looked at the man's face. It was worn and haggard, but at the same time the face seemed familiar. I asked his name, and he was obliged to give it to me. He was Don Phillips. I had heard that name before, but I couldn't recall where or when.

I walked to the bookstore with Don's face vividly fixed in my mind. I couldn't shake his worn and tired features from my memory. For the remainder of the day, I worked and tried to forget about the old man. Later that evening after arriving home, my grandmother called to ask about my new apartment. We chatted for half an hour because my grandmother is my best friend. As we were saying good-bye, I asked to speak to Grandfather.

At first, our conversation was the usual talk about how he was doing and how things were on the farm. I knew that my grandfather had lost a close friend a few weeks ago and was still morose; however, he said he was feeling better. I had never met his best friend or known his name. However, as we talked, the name of his friend came out and, astonishingly, his name was Don Phillips. For a brief minute, I paused and reflected again on what had occurred that morning.

I told Grandfather about the man who said his name was Don Phillips. He found it quite odd that there would be another man in our small town with the same name. Nevertheless, he told me to put the incident behind me because a man with the same name was possible. I promised I would, and we said good-bye.

That night I tossed and turned because I knew the man I had met that morning was someone from my past. I wanted answers, but I didn't know how I would get them. I would have to wait for Grandfather to **relinquish** his grief over his lost friend. In the meantime, I thought it would be inappropriate to ask further questions about Grandfather's friend. However, the way Grandfather described his friend matched the description of the Don Phillips I had met that day. How strange, I thought.

Name ______________________ An Unusual Day

Read each question. Circle the letter beside each correct answer.

1. A conclusion one might draw concerning Don Phillips is:
   A. Grandfather's friend actually did not die and is still living in the town.
   (B.) Grandfather's friend did die, and the stranger the speaker meets is just someone with the same name.
   C. The speaker misunderstood the old stranger she met on the street.
   D. The old man the speaker meets is suffering from a mental illness, and whenever he meets someone he always gives a different name.

2. Another word that means the same as the word "morose" is:
   A. sick B. crazy
   (C.) sad D. happy

3. "I looked at the man's face. It was worn and haggard, but at the same time the face seemed familiar." A context clue that might suggest the meaning of the word "haggard" is:
   (A.) worn B. dirty
   C. handsome D. clean

4. Where did the speaker meet the stranger with the name Don Phillips?
   A. at the bookstore one morning
   B. at Grandfather's house
   (C.) on the street on the way to work
   D. at the university one day

5. Which one of the following statements is not true?
   A. The speaker lives three blocks from the bookstore.
   B. The speaker's grandfather lives on a farm.
   C. The speaker has a grandmother and a grandfather.
   (D.) The speaker is a part-time student and works at a job part-time.

6. A word or expression that means the opposite of the word "relinquish" is:
   A. surrender (B.) keep
   C. give up D. offer

7. The first thing the speaker noticed after bumping into the stranger was:
   A. the stranger's neck
   (B.) the stranger's face
   C. the stranger's clothes
   D. the stranger's broken arm

Total Problems: Total Correct: Score:

Name ______________________ Shocking Mistake

Read the passage and answer the questions on the following page.

Shocking Mistake

It was an early summer morning in August, and Mark Williams hurriedly threw his things into his bag. He was getting ready to leave his small North Carolina town for college, and he was overly excited about his newfound freedom. Mark and his best friend Cory planned on attending New York University together. There, they hoped to become experts in a medical field and eventually have a practice of their own. The two college freshmen also wanted to have the time of their lives.

"Mark, are you ready?" his mom yelled from the bottom of the stairs. "Cory's waiting."

About that time, Mark came jolting down the stairs. "Bye, Mom. I love you," Mark said as he gave his mom a big bear hug. "Let's go, Cory," he finally said with an eager look on his face. Then the two jumped into Cory's convertible and were on their way.

Many hours later, after some intense driving, they arrived at New York University. The enormous buildings that blanketed the campus astonished and overwhelmed the new college students, and they could not wait to get to the place where they would be living for the next four years. After a quick registration, they decided it would be wise to find their dormitory room because it was getting late.

Mark removed a tiny slip of paper from his wallet, which read *1407 Maple Lane.*

"That should be easy enough," Mark said to Cory. "We're already on Maple Lane. All we have to do is find the building." They drove down the street approximately ten blocks before coming upon a small sign in a yard which read *1407 Maple Lane.*

"Wow!" Cory exclaimed.

"This must be an awesome dorm!" Mark agreed. They pulled into the entrance, and the colossal gates opened wide, allowing them to enter. Cory drove slowly around the circular driveway and came to a stop at the front door. As they stepped out of the car and walked hesitantly through the large, wooden doorway at the front of the building, both of the boys were overcome with an **eerie** feeling. Darkness fell around this building and there was only a minute amount of light at various points in the corridor. Sensing that it was too late to officially check in, they explored a long hallway and decided that this was a wing of bedrooms. Finding a suitable spacious bedroom, Mark and Cory decided to get some rest, since they had been terribly busy all day.

Both fell into a deep sleep until about midnight when they were awakened by footsteps. They decided to investigate and possibly meet some other students who were probably coming in from a late night date. Rushing downstairs, they were **bewildered** to see an older man and woman in their pajamas in the kitchen. Even more so, the older couple were startled to see the boys.

After some immediate verbal reactions and responses, amidst a threat from the older man, the boys quickly discovered they were not in the college dormitory. They had made a big mistake and were supposed to be at 1107 Maple Lane, not 1407.

Name ______________________ Shocking Mistake

Read each question. Circle the letter beside each correct answer.

1. The main idea of this story might be:
   A. Registering for college for the first time is exciting.
   B. Drive carefully when you are away from home.
   (C.) It is important to pay close attention to details and directions.
   D. Leaving home for college after high school can be fun.

2. A synonym for the word "bewildered" is:
   (A.) puzzled
   B. angry
   C. scared
   D. happy

3. Why were Mark and Cory leaving North Carolina?
   A. to go on a vacation
   B. to go on a business trip
   C. to visit their grandparents
   (D.) to go to college

4. Referring to the sentences: "As they stepped out of the car and walked hesitantly through the large, wooden doorway at the front of the building, both of the boys were overcome with an eerie feeling. Darkness fell around this building and there was only a minute amount of light at various points in the corridor,"—the context clues for the meaning of the word "eerie" are:
   A. around this building
   (B.) darkness fell ... only a minute amount of light
   C. as they stepped out
   D. walked slowly

5. What address were Cory and Mark supposed to find?
   A. 1407 Maple Lane
   B. 1107 Mableton Lane
   (C.) 1107 Maple Lane
   D. 1407 Marble Lane

Total Problems: Total Correct: Score:

Name ______________________ Dyslexia/Archaeology

Read the passages. Circle the letter beside each correct answer.

Dyslexia

People with dyslexia often have difficulty distinguishing the smallest sound unit of language, the phoneme. Because of this handicap, they are frequently unable to connect letters with sounds, distinguish between sounds or separate the different parts of a word. And, they and often mix word parts together. Word omission when reading or writing is another common symptom associated with those having dyslexia. Nonetheless, this is often overlooked as simply being grammatical errors that could easily be corrected. The same goes for those people who confuse letters in many words while in the process of reading or writing. Reversals may be the most well-known symptom of this disorder, although it is commonly not present in its victims. Reversals occur when a person writes or reads backwards. This also carries over into math, where numbers could be transposed in a problem, causing it to be incorrect. Generally speaking, poor spelling and poor handwriting tend to accompany these previously described symptoms.

1. Which of the following statements is false?
   A. People with dyslexia are unable to connect letters with their sounds.
   B. Reversals occur when a person writes or reads backwards.
   (C.) Reversals may be the least well-known symptom of dyslexia.
   D. People with dyslexia are unable to separate the different parts of a word.

Archaeology

Archaeology is the study of objects left by earlier people, including artwork, buildings, clothing, pottery, and tools. Archaeologists trace the development of cultures by studying the things those people made and used. Such objects help them determine what early social life may have been like. Archaeologists are able to study an artifact at a site and piece together an entire way of life for those people who left it behind. Archaeologists study techniques for finding, excavating, dating, and analyzing material remains of past societies, as well as major trends in cultural evolution. They try to pinpoint a particular time and place as gleaned from the artifacts and fit them into a bigger picture of what life would have been like.

2. Which of the following statements is true?
   A. Archaeologists study the development of languages over a period of time.
   B. Archaeologists paint pictures of how they perceive life to be.
   C. Archaeology is the study of animals and plants.
   (D.) Archaeologists study major trends in cultural evolution.

Total Problems: Total Correct: Score:

Name ______________________ **Jazz Music/Capital Punishment**

Read the passages. Circle the letter beside each correct answer.

Jazz Music

At the beginning of the twentieth century, fully developed jazz music emerged. New Orleans, Louisiana was the musical home of the first notable players of jazz, including Louis Armstrong and Jelly Roll Morton. In 1917, the Original Dixieland Jazz Band was the first jazz band to record their music. Mamie Smith recorded in 1920, and these recordings of ragtime, blues, and jazz popularized the music to the public. The 1920s have been referred to as the Jazz Age. Commercial radio stations played live performances. New Orleans, Memphis, St. Louis, Chicago, and New York City were all thriving jazz centers. A lot of musicians from New Orleans migrated to Chicago and then to New York City. As jazz advanced from relatively simple music played by people who often could not read music to a more sophisticated form, large groups of jazz musicians began to play together. This was modeled after society dance bands, forming the popular big bands of the 1930s, leading to the "swing" era.

1. Which one of the following statements is true?
   - A. New York was the musical home of Louis Armstrong.
   - B. The 1930s have been referred to as the Jazz Age.
   - C. Memphis and New Orleans were thriving jazz centers.
   - D. In 1927, the Original Dixieland Jazz Band was the first jazz band to record.

Capital Punishment

Capital punishment refers to the execution of a person found guilty of a very serious (or capital) crime. There are several forms of execution that are used. Though lethal injection is becoming the method of choice, the electric chair and the gas chamber are both still used. For most of American history, the death penalty has been a state and local issue. Criminals are tried and convicted depending on local laws and customs. In 1968, few Americans supported the death penalty. Many people believed the death penalty would be permanently abolished. Between the 1980s and 1990s, more people in the United States began to support capital punishment.

2. The word "capital" in "capital punishment" refers to the word(s):
   - A. guilty
   - B. serious
   - C. lethal injection
   - D. electric chair

Total Problems: Total Correct: Score:

Name ______________________ **Oprah Winfrey**

Read the passage and answer the questions on the following page.

Oprah Winfrey

Oprah Winfrey was born into poverty in the state of Mississippi on January 29, 1954. Her parents meant to name her Orpah after a woman in the Bible, but they misspelled it. In Oprah's early teens she moved to live with her mother in Milwaukee. At the age of fourteen, she was forced to move in with her father in Tennessee or be sent to a "home."

Her father instituted strict discipline, which turned Oprah's life around for the better. At the age of nineteen, she went to work at a local radio station as a reporter and enrolled in Tennessee State University to study speech and performing arts. In 1978 she went to work for a chat show in Baltimore—"People Are Talking." The management stated that they did not really know what to think of her. However, the viewers loved her and the show's ratings reflected it.

In 1984 she accepted a job as a host of *A.M. Chicago*, which was scheduled opposite of Phil Donahue's top-rated national talk show. Within months Oprah's show was in close competition with Donahue's. Her open and casual style contrasted with that of Donahue's strict formal method.

Oprah received a part in Steven Spielberg's movie *The Color Purple* for which she won an Oscar for best supporting actress. The publicity from the movie launched her show to a national level now called *The Oprah Winfrey Show*. During her first year, the show grossed over $120 million, but she herself only received $30 million. She began a company called Harpo Productions (Oprah spelled backwards) and eventually bought her program from ABC. In 1996, Oprah's show brought in an estimated $97 million.

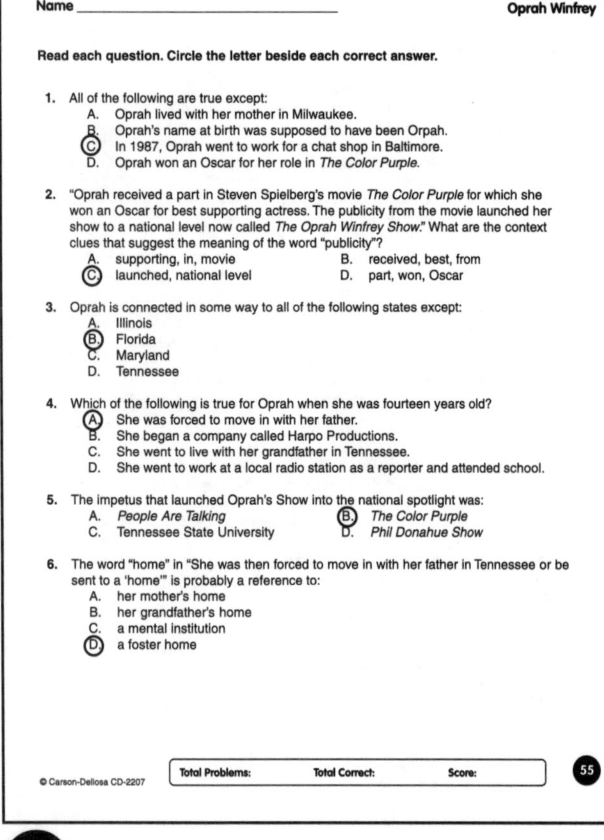

Name ______________________ **Oprah Winfrey**

Read each question. Circle the letter beside each correct answer.

1. All of the following are true except:
   - A. Oprah lived with her mother in Milwaukee.
   - B. Oprah's name at birth was supposed to have been Orpah.
   - C. In 1987, Oprah went to work for a chat shop in Baltimore.
   - D. Oprah won an Oscar for her role in *The Color Purple*.
2. "Oprah received a part in Steven Spielberg's movie *The Color Purple* for which she won an Oscar for best supporting actress. The publicity from the movie launched her show to a national level now called *The Oprah Winfrey Show*." What are the context clues that suggest the meaning of the word "publicity"?
   - A. supporting, in, movie
   - B. received, best, from
   - C. launched, national level
   - D. part, won, Oscar
3. Oprah is connected in some way to all of the following states except:
   - A. Illinois
   - B. Florida
   - C. Maryland
   - D. Tennessee
4. Which of the following is true for Oprah when she was fourteen years old?
   - A. She was forced to move in with her father.
   - B. She began a company called Harpo Productions.
   - C. She went to live with her grandfather in Tennessee.
   - D. She went to work at a local radio station as a reporter and attended school.
5. The impetus that launched Oprah's Show into the national spotlight was:
   - A. *People Are Talking*
   - B. *The Color Purple*
   - C. Tennessee State University
   - D. *Phil Donahue Show*
6. The word "home" in "She was then forced to move in with her father in Tennessee or be sent to a 'home'" is probably a reference to:
   - A. her mother's home
   - B. her grandfather's home
   - C. a mental institution
   - D. a foster home

Total Problems: Total Correct: Score:

Name ______________________ **Eldrick "Tiger" Woods**

Read the passage. Circle the letter beside each correct answer.

Eldrick "Tiger" Woods

Eldrick "Tiger" Woods was born on December 30, 1975. He is the son of Earl and Kultida Woods. He was nicknamed "Tiger" after a friend of his father's from Vietnam, Vuong Phong, whom his father had also given that nickname. He was raised in the town of Anaheim, California. Earl Woods believed that his son was special from birth. He noticed that Tiger would sit in the garage and watch Earl hit golf balls into a net. So, by the time he was old enough to get out of the high chair, Tiger had a golf swing.

There was no one who doubted Tiger's skill when Tiger showed them that he could play golf. By age 3, Tiger could shoot 48 for nine holes and appeared in *Golf Digest* at age 5. He won the Optimist International Junior tournaments six times at ages 8, 9, 12, 13, 14, and 15. He also won the Insurance Youth Golf Classic at age 14, when he was the youngest ever to win that title. He won his first U.S. Junior Amateur the next year, 1991, and had seven additional victories. Two years later he had achieved seven more titles, including two U.S. Junior Amateurs. In 1994 he was selected as man of the year by *Golf World*.

Tiger attended Stanford University, and in his second year he had eight victories in 14 tournaments and finished lower than third only twice. He was then chosen for the Fred Haskins and Jack Nicklaus College Player of the Year awards. Then, in his junior year of college, he dropped out to become a professional golfer.

1. At 14, Tiger was the youngest golfer ever to win the:
   - A. U.S. Junior Amateur Contest
   - B. Optimist International Junior Tournament
   - C. Insurance Youth Golf Classic
   - D. *Golf Digest* award
2. All of the following are true except:
   - A. Tiger Woods won the Optimist International Junior Tournament six times.
   - B. In 1993, Tiger was selected man of the year by *Golf World*.
   - C. By age 3, Tiger could shoot 48 for nine holes.
   - D. Tiger dropped out of college his junior year to become a professional golfer.

Total Problems: Total Correct: Score:

Name ______________________ The Golden Retriever/Vitamin A

Read the passages. Circle the letter beside each correct answer.

The Golden Retriever

The golden retriever is an intelligent, well-built dog with a golden, wavy coat. It is a truly superior hunting dog with a highly developed sense of smell and great intelligence, which makes it easy to train. The dog is also known for its endurance, excellence in swimming, and ability to retrieve. Its calm, gentle, loyal, and sensitive nature makes the dog an ideal family companion. It is a popular contender in obedience circles and has gained recognition as a guide dog for the blind in recent years. The golden retriever is a symmetrical, powerful, active dog—not clumsy. It is very alert and self-confident.

1. Which one of the following statements is not true?
   (A) The golden retriever is a symmetrical, yet clumsy dog.
   B. The golden retriever is a great hunting dog with a great sense of smell.
   C. The golden retriever is an excellent swimmer.
   D. The golden retriever is used as a guide dog for the blind.

Vitamin A

Vitamin A, one of the first vitamins discovered, is required for a healthy immune system, vision, growth, and reproduction. Perhaps the best known role of vitamin A is its effect on vision. Vitamin A forms a pigment in the eye called visual purple that is required for night vision. Vitamin A is very effective in increasing resistance to diseases and infections. Population studies in developing nations have demonstrated that vitamin A reduces death by increasing resistance to infections. In addition, vitamin A increases the production of antibodies and various disease-fighting cells. With those factors, vitamin A supports a healthy immune system and is also very effective in fighting against cancerous cells. It blocks cancerous cells in cultures and even blocks malignancy in animals exposed to cancer-causing agents. Therefore, vitamin A can be referred to as the wound-healing vitamin.

2. Vitamin A does all of the following except:
   A. support a healthy immune system and work effectively in fighting cancerous cells
   B. increase the production of antibodies and various disease-fighting cells
   (C) build healthy red blood cells
   D. form a pigment in the eye called visual purple

Total Problems: Total Correct: Score:

Name ______________________ Nashville: "Athens of the South"

Read the passage. Circle the letter beside each correct answer.

Nashville: "Athens of the South"

Located on the Cumberland River in the north central part of the state, Nashville, the capital of Tennessee and home of the Grand Ole Opry, is a frequent stop for tourists. Nashville was actually founded in 1779 as Fort Nashborough in honor of the Revolutionary War General Francis Nash. It was renamed Nashville in 1784.

Because of its many educational institutions and numerous buildings constructed in the Greek Revival style, Nashville has been called the "Athens of the South." A replica of the Athenian Parthenon, built in 1897, commemorates Tennessee's statehood.

Among the city's institutions of higher learning are Vanderbilt University and Fisk University. East of the city is The Hermitage, home-place of the nation's seventh president, Andrew Jackson. During Jackson's lifetime, The Hermitage was known as a place of Southern hospitality. Today, the tradition continues as The Hermitage opens its doors to over 250,000 visitors annually.

An important manufacturing center, Nashville produces chemicals, food products, shoes, machinery, automobile glass, metal products, apparel, textiles, and airplane parts. The city has the nation's second largest recording industry and produces the largest volume of country music records. Nashville is also a major publishing center, particularly for religious literature.

1. Nashville has:
   (A) one of the major publishing centers, particularly for religious literature
   B. numerous buildings constructed in the Roman Revival style of architecture
   C. the home of the nation's seventeenth president
   D. the nation's largest recording industry

2. An important manufacturing center, Nashville produces all of the following except:
   A. metal products
   B. airplane parts
   C. automobile glass
   (D) tractor tires

3. The popular entertainment home for country music in Nashville is:
   A. The Hermitage
   B. Athenian Parthenon
   (C) The Grand Ole Opry
   D. Fort Nashborough

Total Problems: Total Correct: Score:

Name ______________________ Hong Kong, China

Read the passage. Circle the letter beside each correct answer.

Hong Kong, China

Hong Kong is situated about ninety miles southeast of Canton, China. Hong Kong was a colony of Great Britain until July 1, 1997, when the Chinese government took control of the city. It has one of the highest population densities in the world (5,412 persons per square mile). About 98% of the population of 6.7 million are Chinese. Most of the people in Hong Kong work in factories, the shipping industry, or for the government. About 60,000 Hong Kong residents emigrate each year, mostly to North America and Australia, seeking better economic opportunities.

Hong Kong was originally acquired by Great Britain because of its magnificent natural harbor (Victoria Harbor). During the nineteenth century, it was the main **entrepôt** for Western commerce with China. One-third of China's imports and exports still pass through the port. Hong Kong's success in exporting manufactured goods to Europe and North America attracted substantial investment by American and Japanese firms. Leading exports are now textiles and clothing, electronics, clocks and watches, domestic appliances, and plastics.

Hong Kong lies just below the Tropic of Cancer. The summer months are hot and humid with a mean temperature of 86°F. Typhoons sometimes occur during this season. The winter months are cooler with a mean temperature of 60°F.

1. Under whose protection and government was Hong Kong until 1997?
   A. China
   B. Australia
   (C) Great Britain
   D. United States

2. Which one of the following statements is true?
   A. About 90% of the population of 6.7 million are Chinese.
   (B) Hong Kong was originally acquired by Great Britain because of its natural harbor.
   C. The summer months are hot with a mean temperature of 80°F.
   D. Hong Kong has one of the lowest population densities in the world.

3. Another word for "entrepôt" is:
   (A) intermediary center of trade and shipping
   B. enterprise
   C. entrepreneur
   D. porter

Total Problems: Total Correct: Score:

Name ______________________ Preparing Banana Pudding

Refer to the recipe to answer the questions. Circle the letter beside each correct answer.

Preparing Banana Pudding

1/2 cup sugar
2 tablespoons all-purpose flour
1/4 teaspoon salt
2 cups milk
3 large eggs, separated
1 teaspoon vanilla extract
1 (12-ounce) package vanilla wafers
4 large bananas
1/4 cup sugar
1/2 teaspoon vanilla extract

Combine the first 3 ingredients in the top of a double boiler; gradually add milk, stirring well. Bring water to a boil; reduce heat to low, and cook, stirring constantly, until mixture is thickened. Beat egg yolks at medium speed until thick and pale. Gradually stir about one-fourth of hot mixture into yolks; add to remaining hot mixture; stir constantly. Cook over low heat, stirring constantly, for 5 minutes or until mixture is thickened. Remove from heat; stir in 1 teaspoon vanilla. Cool for a few minutes. Layer one-fourth of vanilla wafers in an ungreased, 3-quart baking dish. Slice 1 banana, and layer over wafers. Pour one-fourth of custard mixture over the banana slices. Repeat layers 3 times, using remaining vanilla wafers, banana slices, and custard mixture. Beat egg whites at high speed until foamy. Gradually add 1/4 cup sugar, 1 teaspoon at a time, beating until stiff peaks form and sugar dissolves (2 to 4 minutes). Add 1/2 teaspoon vanilla, beating well. Spread meringue over custard, sealing to edge of the dish. Bake, uncovered, at 350° for 20 minutes or until lightly browned. Servings: 6 to 8

1. What is the first thing you do?
   A. Beat the yolks at medium speed.
   B. Bring water to a boil.
   (C) Combine the first 3 ingredients.
   D. Gradually add milk, stirring well.

2. After adding 1/4 cup sugar, what do you do next?
   A. Spread meringue over the custard.
   (B) Beat until stiff peaks form.
   C. Bake for 20 minutes.
   D. Slice one banana and add slowly.

3. How many minutes do you bake the banana pudding?
   (A) 20 minutes
   B. 2 to 4 minutes
   C. 3 minutes
   D. 5 minutes

4. What does "extract" mean in "vanilla extract"?
   A. the outermost or farthest point
   B. to infer or estimate
   C. very unusual; exceptional
   (D) concentrated substance from food

Total Problems: Total Correct: Score:

Name ______________________ Chocolate Lovers' Brownies

Refer to the recipe to answer the questions. Circle the letter beside each correct answer.

Chocolate Lovers' Brownies

Brownie Ingredients
2 cups sugar
1 cup butter, softened
4 eggs
4 1-ounce squares unsweetened chocolate, melted and slightly cooled
$2^1/_2$ cups sifted flour
$^1/_4$ teaspoon salt
$^1/_4$ teaspoon baking powder
2 teaspoons vanilla extract
1 cup broken walnuts or pecans

Glaze Ingredients
6 tablespoons butter
1 cup semisweet chocolate chips
2 teaspoons vanilla extract

Preheat the oven to 350°. In a large bowl, cream together the sugar and butter until fluffy. Beat in eggs until well blended; add melted chocolate. Sift the flour, measure, then sift again with the dry ingredients and add to the creamed mixture along with vanilla and nuts. Spread in a greased and floured 9" x 12" baking pan and bake for 25 to 30 minutes or until no imprint is left when touched with finger. Do not overbake.

If a glaze topping is desired, combine the butter and chocolate chips in the top of a double boiler; add vanilla and blend thoroughly. Pour gently over the brownies and spread by tipping the pan. Cut when cool, as interiors are still moist when fresh from the oven. Yield: 24 brownies

1. What is the first step in the recipe?
   - (A) Preheat the oven to 350°.
   - B. Sift the flour, measure, then sift again.
   - C. Beat in the eggs until well blended.
   - D. Cream together the butter and sugar.
2. All of the following ingredients are needed except:
   - A. 2 cups sugar
   - B. 1 cup butter
   - (C) 1 cup marshmallows
   - D. 1 cup broken walnuts or pecans
3. After the eggs are blended, you should:
   - A. Sift the flour.
   - B. Spread in a greased baking pan.
   - C. Preheat the oven to 350°.
   - (D) Add the melted chocolate.
4. This brownie recipe will make:
   - A. 12 brownies
   - B. 25 brownies
   - (C) 24 brownies
   - D. 30 brownies

Total Problems: Total Correct: Score:

Name ______________________ Macaroni and Cheese Casserole

Refer to the recipe to answer the questions. Circle the letter beside each correct answer.

Macaroni and Cheese Casserole

$1^1/_2$ cups macaroni, uncooked
2 tablespoons butter or margarine
2 tablespoons all-purpose flour
1 cup milk
1 cup shredded, processed American cheese
$^1/_4$ teaspoon salt
$^1/_4$ teaspoon pepper
$1^1/_2$ cups **diced** cooked ham
2 tablespoons prepared horseradish
2 teaspoons prepared mustard

Cook the macaroni according to the package directions; drain and set aside. Melt butter in a heavy saucepan over low heat; add flour, stirring until smooth. Cook 1 minute, stirring constantly. Gradually add milk; cook over medium heat, stirring constantly, until mixture is thickened and bubbly. Add cheese, salt, and pepper, stirring until cheese melts. Stir in ham, horseradish, and mustard. Combine macaroni and sauce, stirring well. Pour into a greased 1-quart baking dish. Bake, uncovered, at 350° for 20 minutes or until thoroughly heated. Servings: 4

1. What does the word "diced" mean?
   - A. thrown
   - B. cooked
   - (C) cut
   - D. eaten
2. After draining and setting aside the cooked macaroni, the next step is:
   - A. Cook the macaroni for one minute longer.
   - B. Add flour to a saucepan.
   - C. Add milk and cook over medium heat, stirring constantly.
   - (D) Melt the butter in a saucepan and add flour.
3. How long and at what temperature do you bake the casserole?
   - A. 4 minutes at 350°
   - (B) 20 minutes at 350°
   - C. 20 minutes at 300°
   - D. 10 minutes at 350°
4. The only ingredient not used in the preparation of the macaroni and cheese casserole is:
   - A. all-purpose flour
   - B. shredded, processed American cheese
   - (C) green bell peppers
   - D. butter or margarine

Total Problems: Total Correct: Score:

Name ______________________ San Francisco: The Contemporary City

Read the passage. Circle the letter beside each correct answer.

San Francisco: The Contemporary City

San Francisco, located on the coast of California, occupies a peninsula that is the southern landfall of the Golden Gate channel. This narrow channel connects the Pacific Ocean with San Francisco Bay, one of the world's most beautiful, natural harbors. Spanning the channel is the Golden Gate Bridge, long a symbol of the city as the U.S. port of entry on the Pacific coast.

A popular tourist city, San Francisco offers spectacular views from its forty-three hills. The weather remains mild throughout the year, with average monthly temperatures differing little from January (49°F) to September (64°F).

San Francisco today has an economy very dependent on white-collar industries. A skyline of high-rise office buildings, dominated by the Transamerica Building and the Bank of America tower, marks the downtown **terminus** of Bay Area Rapid Transit (BART), one of the country's most modern high-speed mass-transit systems. On Russian and Nob Hills, stately mansions have been replaced by luxury apartment buildings and hotels. The last three cable car lines, now designated as national historic landmarks, still cross the hills. To the east of Nob Hill lies Chinatown, one of the largest Chinese communities outside of Asia. Fisherman's Wharf, a commercial fishing port established by nineteenth-century Italian immigrants, is now a row of restaurants, souvenir shops, and motels. The Cannery and Ghirardelli Square, once fruit canning and chocolate plants, respectively, now house specialty shops, restaurants, and art galleries. Within San Francisco Bay is the former federal prison, Alcatraz.

1. Which one of the following is not a famous landmark in San Francisco?
   - A. Golden Gate Bridge
   - B. Alcatraz
   - (C) State Capitol
   - D. Fisherman's Wharf
2. Another word that means the same as "terminus" is:
   - A. destroyer
   - (B) end
   - C. continuous
   - D. plan
3. San Francisco has:
   - A. one of the world's most beautiful man-made harbors
   - B. two cable car lines as designated national historic landmarks
   - C. a former federal prison located outside the San Francisco Bay
   - (D) one of the largest Chinese communities outside of Asia

Total Problems: Total Correct: Score:

Name ______________________ Central Park West

Refer to the advertisement to answer the questions. Circle the letter beside each correct answer.

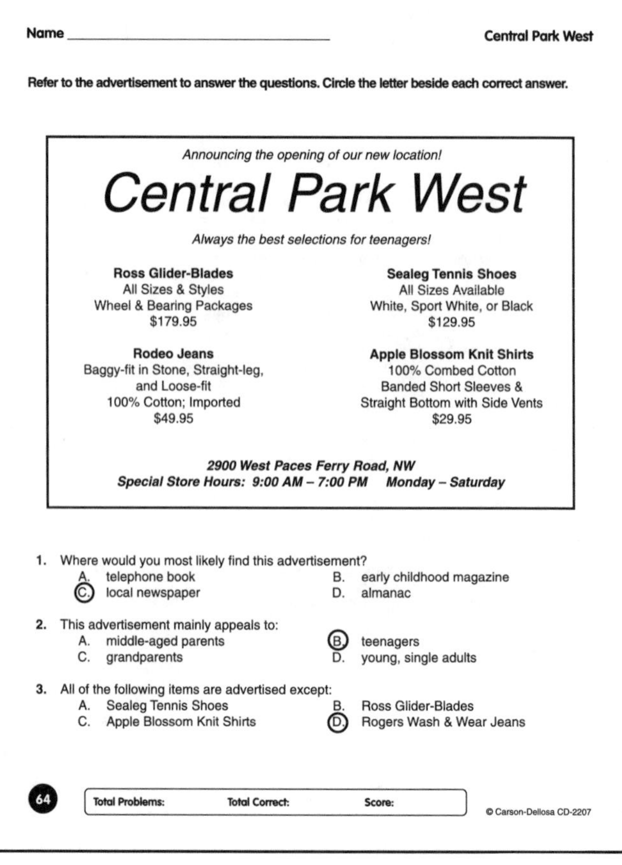

1. Where would you most likely find this advertisement?
   - A. telephone book
   - B. early childhood magazine
   - (C) local newspaper
   - D. almanac
2. This advertisement mainly appeals to:
   - A. middle-aged parents
   - (B) teenagers
   - C. grandparents
   - D. young, single adults
3. All of the following items are advertised except:
   - A. Sealeg Tennis Shoes
   - B. Ross Glider-Blades
   - C. Apple Blossom Knit Shirts
   - (D) Rogers Wash & Wear Jeans

Total Problems: Total Correct: Score:

Name ______________________ **A Southern Spring**

Read the poem. Circle the letter beside each correct answer.

A Southern Spring

Robins and dogwoods out on the lawn,
Green grass and little calves out in the pasture.
Tulips and daffodils springing up everywhere.
Flowering cherry trees and pears adorn the landscape.
Sunrise mornings and sunset evenings
reflect the Earth's bounteous fortunes.
Nature, untamed and wild,
like an eagle soaring freely overhead.
I want to run and play today
beside the creek or river.
I want to catch the wind and drink the rain.
I want to feel the sun and smell the land.
I want to be today.

1. Referring to the line: "Nature, untamed and wild, like an eagle soaring freely overhead,"—because nature is compared to an eagle, the writing technique is called a:
   A. metaphor
   B. simile
   C. personification
   D. pun

2. Another word that means the same as "bounteous" is:
   A. wild
   B. beautiful
   C. abundant
   D. sad

3. The main idea of the poem is:
   A. All the animals and plants in nature are out in the springtime.
   B. Nature is untamed and wild.
   C. The author enjoys living in the South and gardening.
   D. The speaker wants to participate in the new life and beginning of spring.

Total Problems: Total Correct: Score:

Name ______________________ **Reading a Mileage Chart**

Refer to the mileage chart to answer the questions. Circle the letter beside each correct answer.

If you are planning a trip by car, you may want to consult a mileage chart like the one below. To read the mileage chart: 1) Locate one of the cities in the left-hand column. 2) Then, go across that row to the column headed by the other city's name. The number shown is the distance in road miles between the two cities.

Road Mileage	Baltimore MD	Charlotte NC	Detroit MI	Louisville KY	Norfolk VA	Phoenix AZ	St. Louis MO
Baltimore, MD	N/A	435	534	617	232	2,348	845
Boise, ID	2,397	2,359	1,968	1,887	2,546	998	1,629
Cheyenne, WY	1,662	1,624	1,233	1,152	1,811	916	894
Dallas, TX	1,367	1,032	1,211	836	1,353	1,067	631
Fargo, ND	1,362	1,432	933	946	1,549	1,691	861
Memphis, TN	913	628	757	382	899	1,478	285
Washington, DC	36	398	534	615	195	2,350	845
Yosemite, CA	2,900	2,658	2,446	2,313	2,929	685	2,055

1. How many miles is it from Fargo, ND, to Norfolk, VA?
   A. 1,691 B. 1,353 **C. 1,549** D. 899

2. How much farther is it from Yosemite, CA, to Charlotte, NC, than from Yosemite, CA, to St. Louis, MO?
   A. 503 **B. 603** C. 602 D. 703

3. How much greater is the distance from Washington, DC, to Detroit, MI, than from Memphis, TN, to St. Louis, MO?
   A. 349 B. 241 C. 248 **D. 249**

4. How many miles would you travel from Dallas, TX, to Louisville, KY?
   A. 836 B. 946 C. 1,211 D. 353

5. The Kretzmers are traveling from Baltimore, MD, to Phoenix, AZ. The Spencers are going from Baltimore, MD, to Cheyenne, WY. How much farther will the Kretzmers travel than the Spencers?
   A. 686 miles B. 868 miles C. 790 miles D. 680 miles

Total Problems: Total Correct: Score:

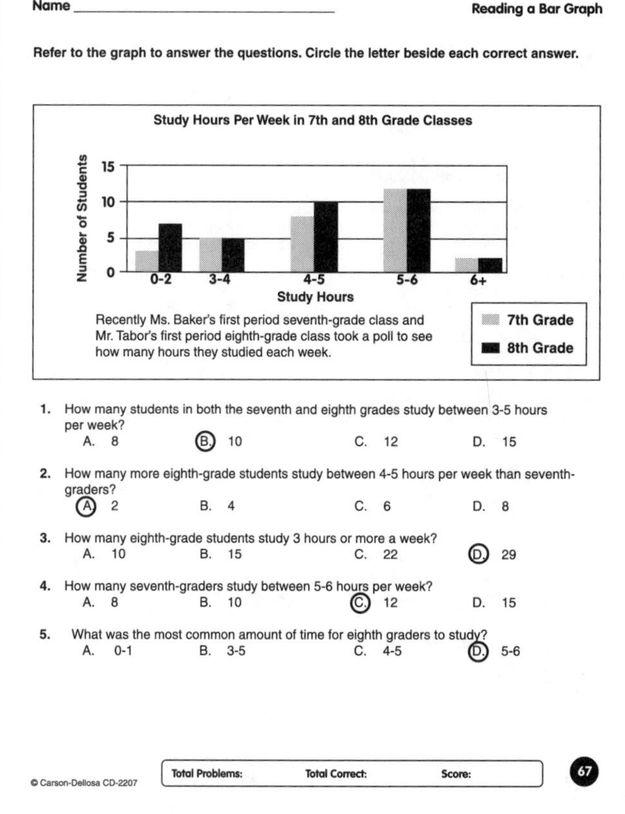

Name ______________________ **Reading a Bar Graph**

Refer to the graph to answer the questions. Circle the letter beside each correct answer.

Recently Ms. Baker's first period seventh-grade class and Mr. Tabor's first period eighth-grade class took a poll to see how many hours they studied each week.

1. How many students in both the seventh and eighth grades study between 3-5 hours per week?
   A. 8 **B. 10** C. 12 D. 15

2. How many more eighth-grade students study between 4-5 hours per week than seventh-graders?
   A. 2 B. 4 C. 6 D. 8

3. How many eighth-grade students study 3 hours or more a week?
   A. 10 B. 15 C. 22 **D. 29**

4. How many seventh-graders study between 5-6 hours per week?
   A. 8 B. 10 **C. 12** D. 15

5. What was the most common amount of time for eighth graders to study?
   A. 0-1 B. 3-5 C. 4-5 **D. 5-6**

Total Problems: Total Correct: Score:

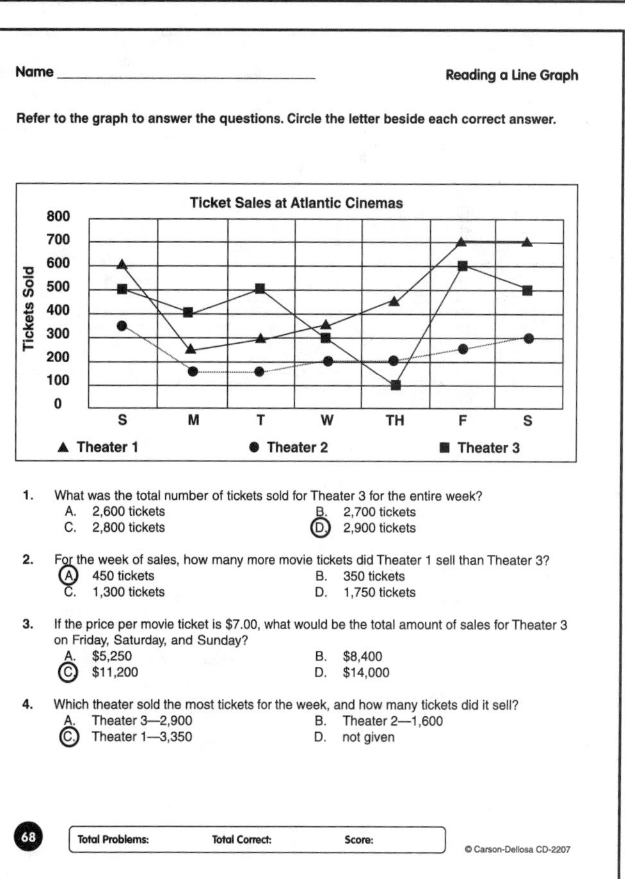

Name ______________________ **Reading a Line Graph**

Refer to the graph to answer the questions. Circle the letter beside each correct answer.

1. What was the total number of tickets sold for Theater 3 for the entire week?
   A. 2,600 tickets B. 2,700 tickets
   C. 2,800 tickets **D. 2,900 tickets**

2. For the week of sales, how many more movie tickets did Theater 1 sell than Theater 3?
   A. 450 tickets B. 350 tickets
   C. 1,300 tickets D. 1,750 tickets

3. If the price per movie ticket is $7.00, what would be the total amount of sales for Theater 3 on Friday, Saturday, and Sunday?
   A. $5,250 B. $8,400
   C. $11,200 D. $14,000

4. Which theater sold the most tickets for the week, and how many tickets did it sell?
   A. Theater 3—2,900 B. Theater 2—1,600
   C. Theater 1—3,350 D. not given

Total Problems: Total Correct: Score:

Answer Key

Name ______________________ **Reading a Pie Graph**

Refer to the graph to answer the questions. Circle the letterbeside each correct answer.

8% 1% 3% 2%
3%
1%

English
Vietnamese
German
French
Japanese
Spanish
Slavic

82%

Languages Spoken at Carmel Middle School

1. If there are 1,500 students attending Carmel Middle School, how many students represent English as their primary language?
   A. 1,150 (B.) 1,230 C. 1,520 D. 1,860
2. How many students represent Slavic, Spanish, and French as their primary speaking languages?
   A. 180 students B. 200 students
   (C.) 210 students D. 220 students
3. If there were 15 more students who speak Spanish and Slavic as their primary languages and you were to subtract that number from the number of students who speak English and Vietnamese, how many students would you have?
   (A.) 1,080 B. 1,045 C. 1,085 D. 1,055
4. If you were to add the number of students whose primary languages are Spanish, Japanese, and German, how many more students speak these combined languages than those of Slavic, Vietnamese, and French?
   A. 50 B. 20 C. 80 (D.) 30

 Total Problems: **Total Correct:** **Score:** 69

Name ______________________ **Reading a Map: Parallels of Latitude**

Refer to the map to answer the questions. Write your answers in the blanks provided.

1. Salem, Oregon is almost directly on the 45° N parallel.
2. The state of Wyoming is located between 41°N parallel and 45° N parallel.
3. Boise, Idaho is south of the 45° N parallel.
4. Denver, Colorado is almost directly on the 40° N parallel of latitude.
5. What city in California is located between the 35°N and 40°N parallels? Sacramento
6. The boundary between Wyoming and Montana is formed by the 45° N parallel.
7. Helena, Montana is in which direction from the 45°N parallel? north

70 **Total Problems:** **Total Correct:** **Score:**

Name ______________________ **Reading a Map: Midwestern United States**

Refer to the map to answer the questions. Circle the letter beside each correct answer.

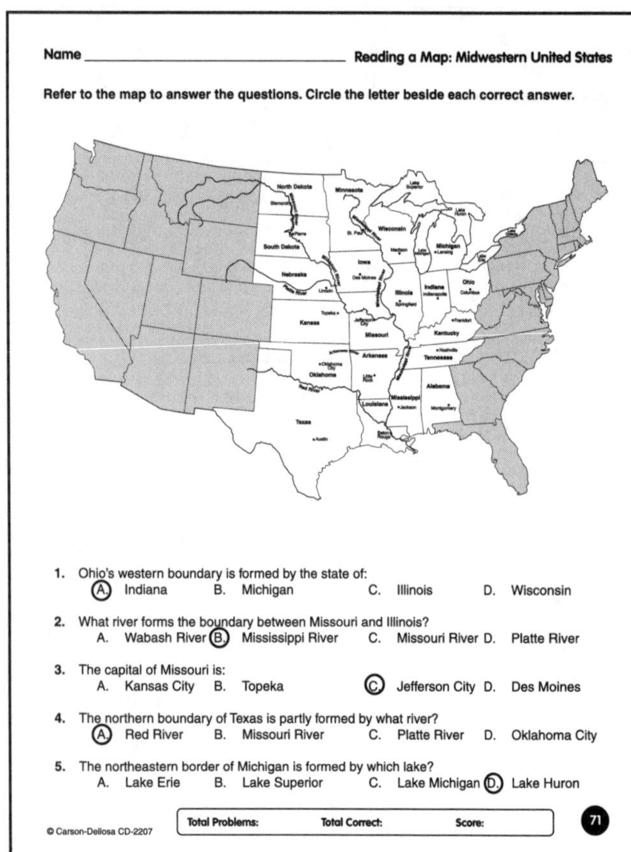

1. Ohio's western boundary is formed by the state of:
   (A.) Indiana B. Michigan C. Illinois D. Wisconsin
2. What river forms the boundary between Missouri and Illinois?
   A. Wabash River (B.) Mississippi River C. Missouri River D. Platte River
3. The capital of Missouri is:
   A. Kansas City B. Topeka (C.) Jefferson City D. Des Moines
4. The northern boundary of Texas is partly formed by what river?
   (A.) Red River B. Missouri River C. Platte River D. Oklahoma City
5. The northeastern border of Michigan is formed by which lake?
   A. Lake Erie B. Lake Superior C. Lake Michigan (D.) Lake Huron

 Total Problems: **Total Correct:** **Score:** 71

Name ______________________ **Library and Reference Materials**

Read each question. Circle the letter beside each correct answer.

Library and Reference Materials

1. If your science teacher suggested that your class plant a corn field in the spring at the right time of the moon, you would consult:
   A. *National Geographic Atlas* (B.) *World Almanac and Book Of Facts*
   C. *Bartlett's Book of Quotations* D. *Reader's Guide to Periodical Literature*
2. In which section of the newspaper would you find movie listings?
   A. sports section B. classified section
   C. front page (D.) entertainment section
3. If you had to find a word that has the same meaning as "dismay," you would look in:
   A. an encyclopedia B. an atlas
   (C.) a thesaurus D. the telephone directory
4. Where in a book do you find the title, author, and publisher (on one page)?
   A. index B. glossary
   (C.) title page D. table of contents
5. If your history teacher asked you to bring in recent information about the secretary of state's most recent political trip abroad, you would probably look in:
   A. an encyclopedia B. a card catalog
   C. a dictionary (D.) a newspaper
6. Your family is going to the island of Crete. You don't know where this island is located. To find out where this island is located, you would probably look in:
   A. a card catalog B. a thesaurus
   (C.) an atlas D. a biographical dictionary
7. You are doing research on the Washington Monument in Washington, DC. To find general information on this famous monument, you could look in:
   A. a thesaurus B. an international who's who
   (C.) an encyclopedia D. Reader's Guide to Periodical Literature
8. Your English teacher asked you to find the meaning of "homonym." You would look in:
   A. an atlas B. a thesaurus
   (C.) a dictionary D. an encyclopedia

72 **Total Problems:** **Total Correct:** **Score:**

Name ______________________________ Reading the Dictionary

Read the dictionary entry below. Refer to the entry to answer the questions. Circle the letter beside each correct answer.

Reading the Dictionary

issue (ish´oo) ***n.*** to go out. 1. an outgoing; outflow. 2. a place or means of going out; outlet; exit. 3. a result; a consequence. 4. offspring; a child or children. 5. profits, as from property; proceeds. 6. a point or matter under dispute. 7. a sending or giving out. 8. the entire amount put forth and circulated at one time: as, the May issue of a magazine, an issue of bonds. 9. in medicine, a discharge of blood, pus, etc. ***v.i.*** {-sued, suing},1. to go, pass, or flow out; emerge. 2. to be descended; be born. 3. to result, as from a cause. 4. to end (in); result, as in an effect. 5. to come as revenue. 6. to be published; to be put forth and circulated. ***v.t.*** 1. to let out; discharge. 2. to give or deal out: as, to issue supplies. 3. to publish; put forth publicly or officially, as periodicals, bonds, and edict, etc. -at issue, in dispute; to be decided. -join issue, to meet in conflict, argument, etc. -take issue, to disagree. -is su a ble, ***adj.*** -is´su er, ***n.***

1. Which numbered definition means "a matter under dispute"?
   A. 2
   B. 8
   (C) 6
   D. 5

2. What is the part of speech for the word "issue" which means "a consequence"?
   A. adjective
   (B) noun
   C. adverb
   D. verb

3. In the following sentence, "The president issued a proclamation announcing that all people would be allowed to vote,"—what part of speech is the word "issued"?
   (A) verb
   B. noun
   C. adverb
   D. adjective

4. What is definition # 2 for the word "issue" used as a transitive verb?
   A. to let out
   B. to discharge
   (C) to give or deal out
   D. to put forth officially

Total Problems: Total Correct: Score:

Name ______________________________ Reader's Guide to Literature

Refer to the Reader's Guide to Literature entry and the sample title page information to answer the questions. Circle the letter beside each correct answer.

Reader's Guide to Literature

Nursing Your Sick Dog [taking care of your dog] R. Schwartz. il *All About Pets* v. 34 no. 14 p. 54-59 O 10 99

1. What is the name of the article in the entry above?
   A. "All About Pets"
   B. "R. Schwartz"
   (C) "Nursing Your Sick Dog"
   D. "Taking Care of Your Dog"

2. Where is the article found, according to the entry above?
   A. Nursing your sick dog
   B. Taking care of your dog
   C. R. Schwartz
   (D) *All About Pets*

3. In which month and year is the article found?
   A. November, 1999
   (B) October, 1999
   C. November, 1954
   D. November, 1959

Title Page

All About Soccer

Terry Payne
Anna Harris

International Publications, Inc.

4. International Publications, Inc., is the name of the:
   A. book
   B. city
   C. author
   (D) publisher

5. Who wrote the book?
   A. Terry Payne
   B. Terry Harris and Anna Payne
   (C) Anna Harris and Terry Payne
   D. Anna Harris

Total Problems: Total Correct: Score:

Name ______________________________ Computerized Card Catalog

Refer to the card catalog entry to answer the questions. Circle the letter beside each correct answer.

Computerized Card Catalog

Title information: Mr. Penn Visits London / by Pat Henry, with introduction by Jorge Fincher

Author: Henry, Pat 1953

Published: London: Red Press, © 1979

Physical description: 214 pp.: 22 cm

Notes: Mark Penn, a newcomer to the big city, becomes the talk of all the young women, until one night an incident happens at a gala event and the identity of young Mark becomes questionable.

Notes: Interest grade level: 7-8

Subject: Humorous fiction

1. According to the card catalog, what do we know about the book?
   (A) The book is about a newcomer called Mark Penn.
   B. Mark Penn dresses as a clown and juggles at a gala event.
   C. At a gala event, a group of rich women discover the true identity of Mark.
   D. One late night a very serious situation occurred at a party.

2. The person who wrote *Mr. Penn Visits London* is:
   A. Pat Fincher
   B. Red Press
   (C) Pat Henry
   D. Jorge Fincher

3. How many pages does the book contain?
   A. 1,979
   (B) 214
   C. 23
   D. 222

4. For what grade level is this book intended?
   A. 6-7
   B. 5-8
   (C) 7-8
   D. 6-8

5. What is the name of the publishing company?
   A. London Press
   B. Jorge Fincher
   (C) Red Press
   D. London Red Press

Total Problems: Total Correct: Score:

Name ______________________________ Reading a Table of Contents

Refer to the table of contents from the book *Ancient Egypt and Greece* to answer the questions. Circle the letter beside each correct answer.

Table of Contents

1. If your teacher asked you to find information on the building of the Great Pyramid of Giza, you could probably find information on what pages?
   A. 19-25
   (B) 6-11
   C. 26-32
   D. 48-53

2. If you were seeking information on the origin of the Olympic Games, in which chapter would you most likely find the information?
   (A) History of the Olympic Games
   B. Greek Statues at Olympia
   C. The Great Pyramid of Giza
   D. Mesopotamia

3. From which chapter would this sentence most likely come? "To protect the mummy from damage, it was placed in a coffin-like container called a sarcophagus. The style, shape, and decoration of the sarcophagus changed over the years."
   A. Ancient Egyptian Burials
   B. Inside the Great Pyramid
   C. The Great Pyramid of Giza
   (D) Mummies

Total Problems: Total Correct: Score:

Name ____________________ **Reading a Memo**

Refer to the memo to answer the questions. Circle the letter beside each correct answer.

Reading a Memo

DATE: May 12
TO: Virginia Powell, General Manager
FROM: Stacie Kendall, Inventory Clerk
RE: Inventory Receiving Report

After checking the receiving report and the inventory in the warehouse, I have found the following **discrepancies** on our recent order:

1 case of notebook paper #017358
2 cases of computer paper #480571
6 packages of blue ballpoint pens #264325
3 cases of third-cut file folders #832109

Please find attached my count, as well as the inventory records.

Attachment

1. What is the item number (#) for the computer paper?
   A. 832109 B. 264325
   C. 017358 (D.) 480571

2. Another word that means the same as "discrepancy" is:
   (A.) inconsistency B. amount
   C. agreement D. addition

3. Who sent the memo?
   A. Virginia Powell B. Attachment
   (C.) Stacie Kendall D. not given

4. The purpose of the memo was to relate information concerning:
   A. stolen goods (B.) inventory
   C. new warehouse D. closeout sale

Total Problems: Total Correct: Score:

Name ____________________ **Reading an Index**

Reading an Index

Refer to the index to answer the questions. Circle the letter beside each correct answer.

Transportation (travel), early settlers, 69; in 1780s, 166-167; transcontinental railroad, 440-441, 458; automobile, 458-461, 488, 740; airplane, 461, 589-591, 691, 693-694; in Alaska, 691; in Hawaii, 693-694
Treasury, Dept. of, 180, 217
Treaty, of 1763 (France and England), 110-111; of 1783 (Paris), 225-226, 253, 753; of 1819 (Spain), 371, 752-753; of Versailles, 548-551,
Trenton, NJ, 143-144, 757, 764
Triangular trade, colonial, 83-84
Triton (submarine), 681-682
Trolley cars, 464, 483-485
Trujillo, General Rafael, 713
Truk, 519
Truman, Harry S, 684-686, 688-689; becomes president, 618, 649-651; decides to use atom bomb, 624-625; and UN, 625; foreign policy, 648-650; Point Four program, 658; Korean War, 661-663; OAS, 673
Truman Doctrine, 656-657
Trusteeship Council, UN, 626-627
Trusts, 492; rise of, 492-493; reform of, 493-497
Tubman, Harriet, 386-388
Tulsa, OK, 757-758
Tunisia, 614-615
Turkey, 538-539, 656-657, 661, 672, 711
Turner, Frederick J., 254
Turnpikes, 273-274
Tuskegee Institute, 431, 721
TVA. See Tennessee Valley Authority.
Twain, Mark, 276-277
Twelfth Amendment, 200, 209-210
Twentieth Amendment, 213-214
Twenty-first Amendment, 214-215, 554
Twenty-second Amendment, 215, 665, 686
Twenty-third Amendment, 215, 686
Twenty-fourth Amendment, 730

1. If you wanted to find information on the atom bomb that was used by a former U.S. president, on what pages would you look?
   A. 753-754 (B.) 624-625
   C. 225-226 D. 658-659

2. If you were researching Hawaii and you wanted to find information on travel in the state, on what pages would you look?
   A. 166-167 B. 69-70
   (C.) 693-694 D. 691-692

3. On what page would you look to find the main office for the TVA?
   A. 721 B. 276
   C. 431 (D.) not given

4. Which one of the following statements about the index is not true?
   A. Information on Harriet Tubman can be found on page 387.
   B. Information on Tuskegee Institute in Alabama is found on page 721.
   (C.) Trolley cars and turnpikes are found on pages 274 and 465.
   D. The Twentieth and the Twenty-fourth Amendments are found on pages 214 and 730.

Total Problems: Total Correct: Score: